LEADERSHIP
IN
MOTION

Leadership in Motion

Laughs, Landed Cost & Lessons That Mattered

Jarrod Kuhn

For information, contact:
Vireo Lex, LLC
San Diego, CA
PR@vireolex.com

This is a work of non-fiction, based on real experiences and events from the author's professional life. Names and identifying details have been changed, and some events have been adapted, merged, or dramatized for clarity, narrative flow, and to protect the privacy of individuals. Any resemblance to actual persons, living or dead, beyond those clearly identified, is purely coincidental.

ISBN: 979-8-218-81905-7
Printed in the United States of America
First Edition: September 2025

All cover and interior illustrations are original works, created under the direction of the author. All artwork is copyrighted © 2025 by Jarrod Kuhn

Book design by Jarrod Kuhn
Set in Garamond
Printed by Vireo Lex Media

To Jillian, Kaitlyn & Andrew—
though the paths in these pages led me far from home, you were
always with me, in my thoughts, in my heart, and in the strength
that I found in being your dad.

To my angel, Jarrod Jr.—
your light remains part of every step I take.

To my lovely wife, Erin—
thank you for believing in me.
this book stands on the strength of your support.

"You don't lead by hitting someone over the head—that's assault, not leadership."

— *Dwight D. Eisenhower (popularly attributed)*
Five-Star General of the Army;
Supreme Commander, Allied Expeditionary Force, WWII;
34th President of the United States.

TABLE OF CONTENTS

CHAPTER ONE

On the Inside: A Vietnamese Sourcing Tale

.... 1

CHAPTER TWO

"You're in China Now": The Phrase That Said It All

.... 29

CHAPTER THREE

Desert Terms: What the Sand Didn't Say

.... 59

CHAPTER FOUR

Three Moves Ahead: A Field-Tested Framework for Change

.... 83

CHAPTER FIVE

Footnotes from the Field: Lessons Learned, Not Taught

.... 123

CHAPTER SIX

Gut, Checked: Felt Before It's Proven

.... 149

CHAPTER SEVEN

Terminal Insights: A Gate to What Comes Next

.... 157

Foreword
by Michael Pacharis, CEO, Lenox Corporation

When Jarrod first asked me to write the foreword to this book, my mind went immediately to the journeys we shared. Journeys that started in airport security lines and ended in factory conference rooms halfway around the world. Journeys where plans met reality, where our best-laid strategies collided with culture, instinct, and circumstance. Journeys that taught us that leadership isn't a title. It's the way you show up when things don't go as planned.

I had the privilege of working alongside Jarrod on many of these adventures. In the book, I appear at times as "Chad," but what matters more than the name is the shared experience. I watched Jarrod turn setbacks, an electrical shock in an airport business lounge, a tough negotiation in Vietnam, or a sourcing puzzle that didn't add up, into moments of clarity, humor, and leadership. He has an uncanny ability to take complexity and strip it down to the essentials: what matters now, what matters next, and how people must be brought along for the ride.

What you'll find in these pages is not a textbook of leadership maxims, but lived wisdom. Jarrod doesn't preach; he tells stories. Stories that will make you laugh, sometimes wince, and often nod in recognition. And woven through each is a practical truth about how to lead, whether across cultures, across functions, or simply across the table.

For me, the greatest lesson I've taken from working with Jarrod is that leadership in motion requires two things: clarity of purpose and agility in practice. You can plan, model, and forecast, but in the end, it's your instincts, your resilience, and your ability to connect with others that carry the day. That's what I saw time and again traveling with him, and it's what he has captured here for you.

So read with curiosity. Let yourself enter the stories. And take what resonates into your own journey. Because while the details may be global, the lessons are universal.

—Michael Pacharis

Preface

The lessons and anecdotes in this book are meant to resonate with anyone who leads, at any level, in any stage of their journey. However, I've found the best way to absorb leadership isn't by collecting advice like items in a basket. It's more like using a filter, sifting ideas through our own experiences and values, to find what truly fits. The most impactful leaders I've encountered didn't offer a one-size-fits-all model. They left impressions, sparked curiosity, and made me want to try something different. Over time, the synthesis of their approaches, combined with my own trial, error, and creative application, became a personal style I could stand behind. That's where I found the gold.

As a lifelong learner, I've rarely been satisfied with what I know. I challenge myself to stay open, to keep seeking, and to absorb leadership insights wherever they come from, whether in the form of a framework, a conversation, or a well-timed failure. Experience has shown me that extraordinary results often grow out of the smallest details, especially when navigating the same challenge again and again with greater precision. In that spirit, I challenge you to find something new here, something to explore or experiment with on your own leadership journey. Count this as one more perspective added to your boundless body of knowledge and experience.

These stories, and the lessons that shaped them, reflect the often-unexpected nature of growth, grounded in real-world experiences that don't always follow the plan.

If there's a particular audience I had in mind while writing, it's those early in their careers in supply chain, logistics, global trade, or international business. If that's you, welcome to a profession where complexity is constant, stakes are high, and clarity doesn't always arrive on time. I've been where you're headed, sometimes confidently, sometimes clumsily, and this book is my way of sharing what I've learned along the way.

This isn't a how-to manual or a comprehensive list of best practices. Even if it were, most of it would be outdated before the ink dried. Leadership benefits from structure, values, and guardrails, but the space between is dynamic. People, cultures, and contexts shift. That's the real subject matter of leadership. What helped me most early on weren't instructions, but perspectives. I would've welcomed a window into what it feels like to walk into a supplier's executive conference room for the first time. How to listen when the translation was fuzzy but the meaning was clear. When to trust my gut, and when to slow down and ask better questions.

As the title suggests, this book follows leadership *in motion*. It assumes a thoughtful plan, one that's well designed, resourced, and supported, but focuses on what happens once that plan is set into motion. The messy part. The movement. The agility it takes to adapt, problem-solve, and lead through the gaps that the best-laid plans never anticipated. Whether its sourcing trips gone sideways or trade negotiations that lean into the unexpected, what follows is a collection of moments from the field, sometimes improvised, sometimes humbling, but always real.

Throughout this journey, I've tried to distill the *lessons that mattered*, lessons about trust, cultural fluency, awareness, instinct, and leadership cadence, the tempo that balances deliberate purpose with timely action. If you're just getting started in global business, I hope these pages offer some context, and maybe a head-start. If you've been in the game for a while, I hope they bring reflection, and maybe a few *laughs of recognition*. If we're having a little fun alongside solid results, that counts as bonus in my book.

Wherever you are on your journey, thank you for letting me be part of it.

—Jarrod Kuhn

Introduction

Transformation

When I began my career in the early '90s, the world of supply chain, strategic sourcing, and logistics was undergoing a powerful transformation. International trade, the lifeblood of nations since antiquity, was about to be supercharged. You could see the shift reflected in how the profession defined itself. In 1985, the National Council of Physical Distribution Management (NCPDM) rebranded as the Council of Logistics Management (CLM), expanding its focus beyond warehousing and transportation to include inventory and procurement. Then in 2004, it evolved again, becoming the Council of Supply Chain Management Professionals (CSCMP), embracing the full spectrum of end-to-end supply chain strategy and execution.

What reshaped these disciplines was a wave of technological innovation, tools designed to plan, analyze, measure, manage and integrate like never before. These powerful advancements were both resourceful and disruptive, unlocking new ways to reduce inventories, automate workflows, and streamline operations. Suddenly, static activities and performance metrics came alive, displayed on dashboards offering a real-time view of a world in motion. The wall map I once used, with plastic tank cars guided by magnets and moved daily based on carrier updates, was, at the time, considered a clever visual approach. Now, a single keystroke confirmed that the tank car was still parked in Ogden, marking day three of its unintended layover.

Enterprise Resource Planning (ERP), Warehouse Management Systems (WMS), Transportation Management Systems

(TMS), and demand forecasting tools blasted onto the scene, bringing business intelligence over enterprise platforms, SQL Server databases, client-server applications, and eventually tools like Smartsheet, Crystal Reports, BusinessObjects, and MicroStrategy. By the mid-2000s, the buzz surrounding *The Cloud* rivaled the AI hype we see today. It promised web-enabled business solutions with pricing amortized across public user domains, lowering barriers to entry and leveling the playing field. Even today's promise of AI owes much of its scale, speed, and data accessibility to the groundwork laid by cloud computing.

As one parcel rep told me at the time, "Customers used to call me for price, now they want my SCAC code" … the Standard Carrier Alpha Code needed to set a carrier up in a TMS. At the same time, globalization was breaking markets wide open. Supply chains stretched farther, and outsourcing overseas became an expanded frontier. Only this time, all eyes weren't on the Wild West, but on the blossoming East. Products stamped Made in Taiwan, Japan, Mexico, and Korea quickly began sharing shelf space with the rising prominence of Made in China, India, Vietnam, or someplace just as cost-effective. Naturally, critics, then as now, voiced concern over the steady drift from Made in USA.

With new systems and new geographies in play, a race was on. Industries and competitors scrambled to seize the advantage, aiming to sell cheaper and profit more. Offshore sourcing became a balancing act, riddled with compromises and trade-offs. One quality manager known at the time said it best, "Quality, service, price… pick any two." Still, the phrase that echoed through meeting rooms, conference stages, and business journals was the same—*Continuous improvement.* Armed with data, empowered by access, and fueled by ambition, we chased the holy grail of global operations, to deliver flawlessly the first time, do it better the next time, and repeat, *ad infinitum*. Concepts like Build to Order (BTO), Make vs. Buy, Just in Time (JIT), Lean, Cross Docking, Direct Store Delivery (DSD), Collaborative Planning, Forecasting, and Replenishment (CPFR), and Six Sigma weren't just talking points, they were either born or reignited to new heights.

Operations pros were no longer just line managers. They spoke Balance Sheets, P&Ls, and Cash Conversion Cycles with fluency. COOs were rising to CEOs, with early examples from Apple, GM, Ford, Dow, and Chevron among those leading the charge. Whole industries were being reshaped by supply chain innovation. Dell's Build-to-Order and Direct-to-Consumer model, for instance, revolutionized how consumers purchased personal computers, just one example among many. It was an exhilarating time to be in supply chain, logistics, or anywhere in operations. Around every corner, something new was emerging or evolving. That constant change? It was magnetic, pulling more people into the action. To put it in perspective, a young Doug McMillon started on the warehouse floor, working his way through the ranks during the '90s and 2000s. By 2014, he earned his spot at the helm of Walmart, then the world's largest company by revenue, at over $450 billion.

Back then, only a handful of universities had begun shifting their operations degrees out of engineering and into their business schools, embracing modern concepts and the emerging disciplines of supply chain management and logistics. A few stood out as early innovators, such as Michigan State University, University of Tennessee, Arizona State University, Penn State University and University of Arkansas. MIT and Georgia Tech evolved into powerful cross-disciplinary hybrids blending the analytical rigor of engineering with the strategic framework of business. All helping to shape the next generation of supply chain professionals. As demand for talent grew, so did the opportunities. Entry-level roles became career pathways. The field attracted pioneers, eager to chase new frontiers across ever-expanding global horizons.

The old ops mantras, like the resigned slogan, *don't worry about the mule, just keep loading the wagon*, began to fade. In their place? Visions of flying Pegasus, carrying just enough, just in time, priced just right. Possibility was taking shape, momentum was building.

New Horizons

As we stand here, 30 years later, I'm reminded that the internet delivered many of its promises, and a few curve balls we never asked for. And yes, I still miss my BlackBerry, or really, any mobile device with hard keys. Enterprise systems never stopped evolving. They became faster, more connected, and always within reach, whether at our fingertips or our thumbs, day or night. Continuous improvement? It never stopped. It still hasn't. From where I sit, technological advancement has been a mixed bag, especially when it comes to staying sharp in business, and even more so on the global stage. The further we drift from being hands-on, in person, and on the ground, the more we risk dulling our instincts. The lingering effects of the global pandemic only makes that distance feel greater.

Yet, I remain convinced, at work and at the end of the workday, what genuinely brings us together, in life and in business, isn't machines. It's lived connection. Forming relationships over collecting followers. Choosing to see things up close and personal, rather than through a distant lens. Being the source of your own influence, rather than chasing someone else's reality. It's from this premise that I'm thrilled to share a few personal stories about what it's truly meant to live and work as a global business professional. In short, the lessons that mattered. After all, where's the fun in virtual reality over screens when you can earn the scrapes and bruises, and painfully feel your way through the real thing?

Now, let's turn the table to you. Whether you're just entering the world of global business or already a rising star, count yourself lucky. If your first international project is on the calendar, pause for a moment and congratulate yourself. Being sent abroad means you've earned trust. You're seen as a valuable investment, an appreciating source of strategic advantage. If this is your first time in the driver's seat, tasked with setting the course for others to follow? You've got this. Right? Of course, you do. Some reassuring things to keep in mind to build your confidence. First, practicing global supply chain, logistics or any international business field sounds exciting, and lives up to those initial impressions. You're essentially thrust into the world, immersed into new cultures and lands. In ancient times you could be mistaken for Marco Polo traveling on the Silk Road. Merchants, traders and explorers of centuries ago are today's sourcing, supply chain, logistics, marketing, product, trade and business development professionals. Then and now, all share some things in common very relatable to the job at hand, a zest for adventure, unquenching thirst for discovery and the resolve to act, not just analyze. Few arrive first. Most follow later.

However, buyer beware! Transacting globally has as many pitfalls as you'd expect from an *Indiana Jones* movie. Like Indy, you're on a treasure hunt, and many things stand in your way, some known, others unimaginable. Maybe the better movie analogy is *Goonies*… You could be challenged under high stakes to play the music that opens the passageway toward richly rewarding results, where others have tried and failed. Or, perhaps you're just going to wing it like *Bill and Ted's Excellent Adventure.* If you're reading this far, I think not. You're more likely focused on outsmarting pirates and outpacing other bounty hunters, though agree with *Ted* on one thing, the next step taken will be *most triumphant.*

As we get started, one important disclaimer. Within the following pages will not be the answers to those earlier mentioned unknowns that you will encounter. Your experiences will be different and all your own. Of course, if I were writing to a younger version of myself, maybe I could offer a perfect treasure map, each step plotted, every detour avoided, success guaranteed without the stumbles. From your unique journey, what you will come to know, will shape your mindset. That mindset will ultimately define the international business professional you become.

With expectations tempered, let's set the stage for what's to follow. The overarching theme that runs through the pages ahead is learned "instinct development." It's not a term that I am claiming credit but one that I believe is neglected, dare I say even in many business school programs. The reality is that finely-tuned instincts play a critical role to being successful, even with all of the latest business intelligence that we now have at our finger tips. You might even say, this is getting back to basics.

How do we develop the secret sauce that will become that magic ingredient, that inner voice, guiding us effectively away from and over the top of obstacles to reach our greatest potential, leading us to repeatable and outstanding results? Spoiler alert, much of it is work that I cannot do for you. There will be pain and suffering, ups and downs, wins and losses, that you will live through and learn from. What I can share are a few bread crumbs, from my own humble missteps, and offer some best practices that I've developed which should have broad application.

Anyhow, you've made it to this point and you've been handed the responsibility and decision-making influence over the PO, poised to conquer new markets. You may even be sporting the overhead-compartment envy of a *Tumi* roller. With or without it, you're ready to roll. One final note before we get started. Even though I referred to the formula of developing your instincts, your "street smarts" so to speak, as a "secret sauce" I would encourage you to spill the beans. Share your victories and defeats with others, to the extent of course you don't violate any corporate confidences. If you're fortunate, you'll receive the same. A mentor of mine was keen to say, "one plus one equals more than two." Meaning that when you network ideas there's a knowledge multiple gained that would essentially be impossible, or take much longer, to duplicate on your own.

Oh, one more thing. Fair warning, you're in for some attempts at comedy. It's not my day job, and some of the punch-lines may be outdated or oddly specific. The goal is simple, to make the journey more enjoyable and share a few hard-earned insights that might just make your own adventure a little easier. If you laugh a bit and take away something relatable, then I've accomplished exactly what I hoped for. Ready for takeoff? I hope you brought a good book.

Your first pearl of wisdom… Don't sleep through the ice cream service mid-flight.

Acknowledgements

This book is the result of far more than my own efforts. It's a reflection of the people I've learned from, worked alongside, and traveled with throughout the years. Across factories, airports, meeting rooms, and border crossings, I've had the privilege of being surrounded by remarkable individuals who've challenged me, taught me, and stood by me.

To the mentors who shared their wisdom, the colleagues who rolled up their sleeves beside me, the interpreters of both language and subtext, and the trusted professional who showed up and delivered, thank you. Your influence runs deep in these pages.

I am especially grateful for those who were willing to share their world with me, whether through a conversation, a partnership, or a gesture that revealed more than words ever could. You've helped me see things I might have missed and made me better for it.

Without the support, patience, and belief of so many, this book, and the career that shaped it, would not exist. I'm humbled by the journey and those who helped guide it.

1

ON THE INSIDE:
A VIETNAMESE SOURCING TALE

A jolt in the airport lounge on the way, a hot muffler somewhere in between, and a flying chair just as it was all starting to come together, this rigorous tour of Vietnam's candle backstage illuminated before our eyes, revealing clues that led us to… the glow behind the curtain. Or, in the words of one wise cabbie, the way to the inside, where hidden value gets uncovered. Set against backdrops that included a Lennon bobblehead in a hula skirt, three watchful dogs, moments of Socrates at the whiteboard, pillars of persuasion, and one masterclass in the cash-flow theory of volume, we accomplished the mission. A full-size die-cast airplane became the unexpected trophy, a reminder that where you finish is almost never determined by where you start. This wasn't just any sourcing trip. It took a blend of theory and practice, grit and bandages, but once again, it proved that the path to the best deals isn't drawn up in the office. It's hammered out on the ground, among the hazards… and the water buffalos.

LIGHTING THE WAY

An experienced Saigon-based sourcing firm had been engaged to assess the supply landscape, make key contacts, and establish inroads to factory-direct sources. Since the '80s, a U.S. antidumping order had remained in force, imposing a 108% duty on wax candles originating from China, with a few exceptions. As a result, many wax candles were being produced in Vietnam and Thailand, often by factories wholly owned or jointly ventured. Most of the opportunity appeared to be blossoming in Vietnam.

Our search spanned Hanoi in the North, Saigon (Ho Chi Minh City) in the South, and Da Nang on the Central Coast, situated between the two. The sourcing firm had gathered enough intelligence to validate our assumption that Vietnam could be viable sourcing ground. Meetings were arranged throughout the country, and before long, we were planning a trip to see for ourselves.

Business visas affixed inside our passports and a full two-week itinerary in hand, my colleague Chad and I, were on our way. Although I had a favorite airline for most of my career, back then, at least for international travel, it was always wise to shop around for the best deal.

This time, it was China Southern Airlines. By this point, I had paid my dues with years of flying "tourist class." Years, mind you, of 12 to 19-hour flights with someone inevitably falling asleep on my shoulder, eliciting more envy than annoyance as I struggled to sleep myself. Welcome to business class. Where the seat reclines a full 180 degrees and sleep is finally within reach.

One lesson I'd learned early on was for those long-haul flights to Asia, late morning departures were the best. They made it easier to adjust and hit the ground running. For instance, Vietnam is fourteen hours ahead of Los Angeles. The total flight time is about 18 hours, usually with a connection in Japan, Taiwan, or Korea. A flight departing LAX at 11 a.m. means you'll land around 10 p.m. the next night in Vietnam. If you sleep naturally during the flight, roughly in sync with your normal bedtime, you'll arrive ready for a nightcap, and the best sleep ever. You'll wake up aligned to local time, rested and ready to win whatever the day throws your way. Unfortunately, for this particular flight to Vietnam we left much later in the evening.

THREE PILLARS AND A PLANE

We connected in Narita, near Tokyo, Japan. Another perk of business class is the access to the airline lounge, a luxury that feels more like a necessity after spending 11 hours on a plane. When we arrived to the lounge, the idea of a shower had never sounded better. While Chad called home, I beelined to one of the private shower rooms.

The hot water was amazing. Feeling human again, I threw on a robe and plugged in the hair dryer. There was a large, lighted mirror in front of me. The room was a bit cramped, so as I waved the hair dryer around, my arm kept brushing against the edge of the mirror. After a few passes without issue—lightning struck.

A jolt of electricity shot up my arm, through my shoulder, and down the right side of my body so intensely that I had to use my other arm to pull myself away from the mirror. I didn't realize it at the time, but apparently, I let out quite a scream. On the other side of the shower room door, well into the seating area of the lounge, Chad, still on the phone with his wife, heard it. "Sounds like someone just got stabbed," he said.

Still a bit in shock, literally, and in the fog of a long day and night of travel, I somehow managed to brush the mirror a second time. Another scream. At this point, Chad didn't need a third scream to put the pieces together. Still on the phone, he told his wife, "It's Jarrod."

By the time he reached the shower room, I was already outside, in my robe, underdressed for that part of the lounge, with my hair a frazzled mess, appearing more *Doc Brown* than myself.

Whether it was the static from the dryer or residual electric current, the sight of me in that moment clearly startled a few nearby travelers. Not long after, the lounge staff arrived. I explained what had happened. They moved my clothes into another room so I could change. Needless to say, I had zero trust in trying a second dryer, even in a different location.

Eventually, I made my way to a more relaxing part of the lounge, but this overwhelming sense of responsibility kicked in. I needed to make sure the staff understood the danger and closed that shower room until it could be repaired. To my surprise, there didn't seem to be any urgency, or even much interest. In fact, it was clear they didn't believe me at all. Whether they thought I was exaggerating or just crazy, I was politely dismissed. Meanwhile, my arm was still numb and tingling, but fueled by adrenaline and jet lag, I felt it necessary to escalate the situation. Chad stayed nearby in case I needed backup.

Soon, a group of three or four staff members in what looked like higher-level uniforms approached. However, after consulting with the original staff, they too wore expressions of disbelief as they came over.

I explained everything in painful detail, how I had brushed the mirror, the electric shock, and the second shock afterward. "I'm no electrician," I said, "but something isn't grounded in that mirror, and it could've been a lot worse."

That's when Chad later said I launched into what he called the *three pillars*, an impressive display of persuasive argument, in his words.

I started with:

Customer Service – "How can you allow another airline customer to go through what I just did, now knowing there's a problem?

Then:

Legal Liability – "You've already got one person injured, fortunately not seriously.

What if it's an elderly person next time? Someone with a heart condition? Or, the current is even stronger?"

And finally:

Moral Responsibility – "Whether you believe me or not, what if I'm right and you do nothing? Don't you have a duty to be sure?"

The argument landed. They closed the room and posted an "Out of Order" sign. Chad and I grabbed something to eat, and soon after, we saw maintenance personnel head straight to the shower area. I felt better, though still a little sore.

Well, as eventful as a layover could be, our time was up. We gathered ourselves and headed toward the lounge exit. Just as we were leaving, a group of what appeared to be airline executives entered and approached us. As it turned out, maintenance had confirmed there *was* an electrical issue with the mirror. The execs apologized, assured us the room would remain closed until safe for use. Mission accomplished. We thanked them and as we said our goodbyes, they insisted on giving us a ride to our gate. Sounded great.

We hopped into the back of one of those airport carts. Sitting on the front seat was a large, die-cast model airplane mounted on a pedestal. One of the execs handed it to me as a gift. Off we went, speeding through the terminal in an airport cart, me holding a shiny metal airplane about the same size as my carryon roller. Curious stares followed us all the way to the gate. We finally said our thanks and goodbyes again.

For the next two weeks, I found a way to carry that metal plane through all of Vietnam and back home. It made it, still in one piece, and today it sits in my home office as a monument to what Chad called "the three pillars argument," and the shock-and-awe experience of the Narita business lounge.

If that's how the trip started *before*, we even arrived in Vietnam, I thought, we were in for quite a ride.

WITH A LITTLE HELP FROM… JIMMY

We arrived in Saigon, or more officially, Ho Chi Minh City. We were on our own to catch a cab. There were plenty lined up outside the airport, and ours looked like a nice enough minivan from the outside. Inside? A full-blown tribute to the Beatles.

The driver loaded our bags into the back, and we settled into the rear seat. The humidity was in full force. The AC was doing its best to keep up. John Lennon took center stage, literally, as a bobblehead in a hula skirt, glued to the dashboard. Behind him, a *Sgt. Pepper's* backdrop revealed troll dolls with pink, blue, and red hair, clearly meant to be Paul, George, and Ringo.

Rope lights framed the interior.

Thankfully, it was broad daylight.

"I am Jimmy," the driver said as he cranked up the stereo. No surprise what we expected to hear. However, it wasn't the Beatles, it was Hendrix. *Purple Haze*. How perfect it would've been, I thought, if *Crosstown Traffic* was playing.

Chad and I, windows down, had our phones out, trying to capture all the sights. A sea of scooters surrounded us, some carrying two, three, even four passengers. No one seemed to have a care in the world, zigzagging through traffic in a two-wheeled ballet that somehow avoided disaster with perfect timing.

THE ROOFTOP BRIEFING

We arrived at our hotel, the Caravelle, located in District One and the heart of downtown Saigon. Immediately visible were the remnants of French colonialism from a bygone era. As we approached, the Saigon Opera House stood proudly on the corner, its ornamental columns looking more Parisian than Southeast Asian. We agreed to quickly settle in and then meet up at the hotel's signature rooftop restaurant and bar, *Saigon-Saigon*. The plan was to review tomorrow's itinerary and unwind.

Saigon-Saigon was wonderfully open-air, with city views, a refreshing breeze, and ceiling fans that helped cool the humid air. Inside, we spotted a cigar shop and were drawn to it immediately. France wasn't the only country to leave its mark here. Ho Chi Minh's apparent ties with fellow communist-in-arms Fidel Castro had also left behind some Cuban influence, one of the more enjoyable residuals being the abundance of Cuban cigars.

With a couple of Montecristo No. 2s in hand, Chad with a scotch, me with a mojito, we toasted the start of the journey.

We had arrived.

Tomorrow, we'd have breakfast with the sourcing firm, followed by visits to several factories. For the evening, we decided to keep things simple, eat on property and stay put. As the sun set, a Latin band began setting up on stage. We were in Vietnam, right? Still, the atmosphere was relaxed and easygoing. We went over our strategy while intermittently catching up on emails, clearing the backlog from our time off the grid during the flights.

Before we knew it, the band launched into their set, and the room came alive. People got up to dance. More guests had arrived, a mix of local business professionals and tourists. We soaked it all in. It felt good to simply relax and unwind, with some unexpected but lively background entertainment after a long journey.

Though the Saigon-Saigon rooftop was still buzzing with energy, we eventually made our way back to our rooms. A great night's sleep awaited, and with it, the start of our quest for candles.

FLAME AND MIRRORS

The sourcing firm had done a great job preparing for the trip. We had a solid lineup, including several factories to visit in person, plus a few other prospects who would meet us over coffee.

Most of the day was spent in a minivan, though. Surprisingly, we weren't going very far. The factories we visited had the look of middlemen, trading companies or agents representing factories, not the source themselves. The pricing confirmed our suspicions.

Something wasn't adding up. One candle in particular raised eyebrows, the humble tea light. After meeting with six different suppliers, it became obvious that every one of them was quoting the exact same price for tea lights, despite wide variations on other candle types like tapers, pillars, and jars. Something was off.

That night, back at our de facto office, the Saigon-Saigon rooftop, we debriefed. We zeroed in on the tea light anomaly. One supplier's rep stood out, named **Minh**, a fast-talking, self-proclaimed "Candle Master of Vietnam." We decided to invite him to dinner the next night and dig deeper.

The sourcing firm had more meetings lined up for us in Saigon. We'd seen enough, but went along, just in case a hidden gem turned up. Meanwhile, we were already thinking ahead to Da Nang.

Then dinner happened. **Minh** lived up to his billing. Over grilled fish and cocktails, he confirmed our suspicion. There was one factory supplying most of Vietnam's tea lights behind the scenes. It had no website, no international presence, and was three hours outside the city. It wasn't accustomed to dealing with foreign-buyers directly, but it had the machines, and the volume.

Da Nang could wait.

CANDLE LAND

The next morning, our minivan rolled up. Minh rode shotgun and we were in the back, fully off-script. However, that's sourcing. You start with a few puzzle pieces, and if you're diligent, the rest begins to take shape.

We finally left the sprawl of Saigon behind. The scooters gave way to rice paddies, then water buffalo, grazing knee-deep in swampy grassland. When we arrived, Vietnam seemed to say, welcome to Candle Land. The factory was legit. It was automated, well-run, and operated by Chinese management. There was a quality lab that would meet U.S. standards. Production lines were in motion, and tea lights ran wall to wall.

Chad and I exchanged a look, then turned to Minh. He smiled. "I told you, I know everything about candles in Vietnam." As it turned out, he wasn't just a rep, he claimed part ownership and was the factory's exclusive trading arm.

"Don't worry about a thing," he said.

We assembled in the conference room. The wax floor had clearly seen years of melted and re-hardened spills, an archaeological layer of candle history. Great setup for wheeled chairs, I thought. Chad and I sat down, carefully.

Around the table with us was Minh, the Chinese GM, and factory reps from QC and operations. Minh translated. The numbers were good, but the math didn't quite add up.

So, I walked to the whiteboard and channeled my inner Socrates. "What's your wax cost per ton? "Price for metal cups?" "Wick cost?" "Tell me how this is made and that is sourced." Minh rattled off answers with ease.

Still, based on the breakdown, the labor and overhead would be half of total costs, a stretch for a location we reached by way of water buffalo. Minh didn't argue. He had that look of someone caught with a hand in the cookie jar, and offering to share. The price wasn't perfect, but we were close.

We asked to see more of the factory. That's when my chair betrayed me. One wheel snagged on a crack in the wax floor. I stood, and the other wheels shot forward. I landed flat on my back. If I had earned any respect at the whiteboard, I lost it with that landing. The room rushed to my aid. I preferred they hadn't. Chad helped me up, and I dusted off what dignity I had left.

The tour continued, tailbone trauma added to the list. The factory was well-equipped for tea lights and votives, but jar candles would take us elsewhere.

THE THREE WATCHDOGS

We said farewell to Minh, for now, and resumed our original plan for Da Nang. One promising supplier awaited us there, named Huy. Unlike bustling Saigon, Da Nang was laid-back, coastal, almost surf-town in vibe. Our hotel leaned into beach resort over business hotel. No complaints. The change of pace was welcome.

We reviewed plans at the on-property restaurant, with seafood and sea breeze aplenty.

Truth be told, tea lights were still on our minds, but we focused on the next day's goal of sourcing jar candles.

The next morning, after coffee, we headed out. No buffalo this time, but plenty of dusty roads, tin roofs, and banyan trees. Huy's facility was remote.

We pulled up to the showroom, a separate building from the factory. The greeting committee arrived, three large dogs of uncertain breed. Not aggressive, but definitely not sold on us.

Luckily, Huy appeared. Khakis, Hawaiian shirt, big smile. The dogs stood down. We had been accepted. Huy's showroom impressed. Seasonal candles, jars, and the tall religious candles you find at vigils and memorials. We began our discussion.

The anticipated challenge? The glass. It had to be machine-made, not blown, and painted on the inside to avoid rubbing off. Wick placement mattered. Huy could handle the filling, but not the glass. We toured the factory. For filling, automation made the grade. We flagged a few process improvement opportunities, particularly around wick insertion. All considered Fixable.

Lunch? Pizza Hut. Somewhere between the irony and the familiarity, we liked Huy even more.

Over slices, he shared his history. He'd been burned by big-name clients in the past. Chad and I knew to take that with a grain of salt, but he was convincing. Either way, we'd have to overcome his risk aversion if we ended up working together. Back at the factory, we stayed a few more hours. The dogs, by the way, stayed on a hilltop, still watching.

We had an idea. We knew a glass supplier in China. If Huy would import the glass, we'd provide specs. He'd handle the filling, wick, and packaging. He was open-minded and this prospective source appeared promising.

HA LONG BURN

We headed north. Next stop was Hanoi. The capital promised a more traditional Vietnamese experience. After settling into the JW Marriott, we headed to the Old Quarter for dinner and to shop for postcards for our wives.

We found a pop-up vendor with several turnstiles. As I flipped through them, I found a great photo of Ha Long Bay. I turned to show Chad, and felt searing pain on my left calf.

Like open flame. I jumped back.

Had I been bitten?

Nope. A moped, with its muffler still hot, had pulled up beside the postcard stand. I was wearing shorts so this meant a skin-melting burn, instantly. A bystander, trying to help, offered to dump his glass of ice water on the burn. As politely as I could in the moment, I waved it off.

I learned the hard way that unbottled water abroad was more gamble than comfort, hardly what I'd trust to mend an open wound. The motorist? Wearing a leather jacket in the sweltering heat, he tipped his flat cap, said nothing, walked his bike forward, and sped off.

I'd just met the Vietnamese *King of Cool.*

I hobbled to a souvenir stand and bought a pair of black socks with Vietnam's national colors. Pulled one over the burn and pressed on. Let's recap: electrical shock (arm), chair fall (tailbone), muffler burn (leg).

We were halfway through the trip, and I was running out of body parts. Chad? Unscathed.

Dinner was Cha Ca La Vong, Hanoi's famous grilled fish with noodles. Spring rolls, a local cocktail for Chad, and Bia Hoi beer for me, which helped the sting in my leg. Back at the hotel, first aid was administered, patched up nicely.

NORTHERN EXPOSURE

The next morning, another factory meeting. A car had been sent for us. Standing in the lobby of a busy hotel, trying to spot a driver we'd never met, like a blind date. A few misfires. Then, "Jarrod?" "Yes. Nguyen?" We had found each other. Just like that, the hardest part of the day was over.

At every turn, the factory we visited on the outskirts of Hanoi offered a different experience. Nothing bad, per se, just a level of formality not commonly seen elsewhere in Vietnam. On the surface, the added structure might suggest better quality control, greater efficiency, and tighter cost management.

On the contrary, bureaucracy can often stifle creativity and introduce a host of other problems. Touring the facility reminded me of China in the early 2000s.

Although China had already been shifting from state-owned enterprises to shareholder-owned corporations for years, there was still a mix of government-run and entrepreneurial factories. You could usually tell which was which by the uniformed guards in the lobby and names that included the municipality, like "Shanghai Glass Company." Ironically, the factories where the government maintained a heavy hand often had less appealing product deliverables.

The candle factory in Hanoi didn't raise any red flags that suggested those same pitfalls. The manufacturing equipment and processes were advanced, and we were especially impressed by the rigorous chemical inspection and testing methods for wax blends.

However, once we sat down to discuss pricing and production capacity, significant gaps became apparent. The factory didn't seem to have much open capacity and appeared heavily committed to European clients and domestic sales. Experience with the U.S. market was limited. We agreed to keep in touch, but at first look, the factory didn't appear to be the right fit. We had traveled north for this one factory visit, more as a way to round out our sourcing geography than anything else, wanting to make sure we didn't miss any potential opportunity. Leave no stone unturned.

Next steps for us included returning to Saigon and Da Nang to continue progressing the tea light and jar candle opportunities.

In the meantime, it was Friday, and we had some downtime ahead for the weekend.

CULTURAL DUE DILIGENCE

How international business travelers spend their off time varies. Some stay in their hotel rooms, grinding through work that could usually wait. Others take advantage of the opportunity to get to know the place they're doing business in, to explore a bit. Having experienced both, I've always leaned toward the latter whenever possible, for a couple reasons. First, the obvious, it's personally enriching to step into the shoes of a tourist and enjoy what others have traveled far to see.

More importantly, it's the truest blend of business and pleasure. Why does this matter? Because the more you understand the local culture in a foreign market, the better equipped you are to understand the people you're doing business with. So, smell the roses, I say. Chad agreed to go exploring, so we started with the local area around us in Saigon.

Our first stop was the War Remnants Museum. Even before entering, the grounds present hardware from the Vietnam War, including a "Huey" transport chopper, fighter jets, bombers, and tanks like the Patton, known for its imposing 90mm gun. Inside, the experience turns much more intimate, offering an unfiltered look at the atrocities of war, told unapologetically through the Vietnamese lens. It was a sobering and thought-provoking visit.

At the museum gift shop, I bought a book on another historic site, the Củ Chi Tunnels, which I wouldn't visit on this trip but would explore a couple of years later. The tunnels are a more than 100-mile underground network used during the war by the 'Viet Cong,' formally known as the National Liberation Front, with a small section preserved for visitors to actually crawl through.

Next, we visited the Jade Emperor Pagoda, where we were greeted by burning incense, dragons carved overhead, and a pond filled with turtles just outside. Inside, we respectfully observed locals engaged in worship, a peaceful, sacred place that offered a moment of stillness. By then, it was time for dinner.

The concierge at the Caravelle Hotel had recommended a popular restaurant nearby, described as a Brazilian-style Rodízio steakhouse, similar to Texas de Brazil or Fogo de Chão, where an all-you-can-eat selection of meats is carved and served tableside from large spits. We would make a quick stop back at the hotel, then head out for what promised to be a memorable meal.

The cab pulled up, and it immediately looked familiar.

It was Jimmy. We were happy to see him.

We jumped in the back and headed off for the short ride back to the hotel. Despite all the Beatles nostalgia in his car, this was the second time he had something else playing.

On this ride, we got a bit of the Eagles' *Hotel California*. Fine by me, I thought. It was shortly after sunset, no rope lights...

maybe next time.

After a quick refresh, we were off again. The restaurant was just as advertised, and clearly a hit with travelers and locals alike. They had studied the concept well. The familiar coaster-style signal was in use. Flip it to the green side, and the meats keep coming; red side up, and it's pause or quits. Chad and I stayed green most of the way. One revealing difference between this place and the Rodízio chains back in the States? The variety. It went well beyond the usual sirloin, ribeye, and lamb. I remember frog legs, quail, and some especially curious pork offerings making the rounds. That was enough for me to turn over *red*.

We used the dinner to recap the first half of the trip, our wins, our misses, and the opportunities starting to take shape. It was clear that the second half, more focused on making deals than discovery, looked promising.

With a couple days left before diving back into the business, we had a brainstorm. How cool would it be to hop over to Siem

Reap, Cambodia, and see Angkor Wat? The iconic Hindu-Buddhist temple complex, more than 900 years old, with its five conical towers I'd seen pictured countless times. That sealed it. We'd book a Vietnam Airlines flight in the morning and make the quick jump to Cambodia.

With that plan in place, we flipped our coaster to red and caught a cab back to the hotel. That's when I realized my book on the tunnels was gone. Bummer, I thought. Not sure where I'd left it. No use chasing it now.

We called it a night with thoughts of the next morning's adventure already in motion.

The flight from Saigon to Siem Reap was short, just over an hour. Upon arrival, we were met with our first unexpected sight, a Dairy Queen inside the airport. We couldn't resist the nostalgic pull. One Blizzard and one hot dog each, comfort food from back home.

It was too late in the day to start exploring Angkor Wat, so we aimed to see as much as possible in a single, ambitious day. Outside, a row of minivan cabs waited. We negotiated our way into one, and that's when we met Tiger, our driver.

I immediately thought the name was cool. Tiger quickly got his bearings and asked about our plans. We told him we had come solely to visit Angkor Wat.

What came next was a deal that made itself. He offered to drop us at our hotel that evening, pick us up in the morning, take us around Angkor Wat, and return us to the airport when we were done. No upfront payment. No fixed price.

Just a handshake agreement. Perfect.

We planned on an early start, 6:00 AM.

Morning came quickly. Chad and I had fully embraced our tourist personas, cameras slung around our necks, dressed in shorts, t-shirts, and walking shoes. Tiger was already waiting. Just past sunrise, we were off.

After buying our tickets, we passed through the gates of Angkor Archaeological Park, and it truly felt like stepping into another era. We climbed ancient stone staircases and wandered sacred temple grounds, taking in as much as we could with the time we had. Tiger picked us up at key points throughout the day, helping us maximize the experience.

We managed to see Bayon Temple, with its massive stone faces and intricately carved battle scenes, Ta Prohm, now known to many as the *Tomb Raider* temple for its role in the Lara Croft film, and Banteay Srei, stunning in its pink sandstone and delicate carvings.

By the end, we were exhausted and exhilarated. The trip had been absolutely worth it. When Tiger dropped us at the airport, we surprised him with a very generous payment for his time, flexibility, and kindness. He had made our last-minute side trip seamless, and unforgettable.

GLOW BEHIND THE CURTAIN

Although it wasn't a restful weekend, it was time well spent. Our first stop Monday morning was back to what we'd dubbed "candle land." The factory had arranged for a car to pick us up, and soon we were on our way.

Upon arrival, we were led back into my favorite conference room. As we settled in, it was clear that new faces had joined for this round. Who we thought was the GM turned out to be head of operations. The real GM, Lan, wanted to meet us. She was Vietnamese and spoke perfect English.

The dialogue ignited from both ends and caught fast. We mapped out order plans, worked through payment terms, and landed on a price that made the entire trip worthwhile. Assuming production samples with our packaging met spec and passed approvals back home, we had just secured our first new candle alliance in Vietnam. We noted that representatives would return to oversee initial production, or we'd send in a third-party QC inspector. They were fully on board.

That evening, Lan hosted a dinner at a place in Saigon we never would've found on our own. It was an elegant array of local cuisine with all the right touches. The Wagyu beef and rice dish was outstanding. A French Bordeaux made its way to the table, a fitting punctuation mark to a successful stop in Saigon.

Soon, we'd be heading to Da Nang to meet with Huy.

IT CAN BE DONE

The next two days were filled with meetings with QC inspectors, both agency and freelance, who might be hired on an exclusive contract basis. It's easy to get swept up by cost savings and the polished façade of factories putting their best foot forward.

Actually, though, receiving consistent, spec-meeting goods is a different game. That takes intent. Reagan's "trust but verify" mantra fits well here. With the right unbiased controls, you can avoid tricks of the trade, like *salting*, where a factory shows off a few perfect units to mask broader defects, or its cousin, *peppering*, where subpar items are slowly added over time to make up for quality-related losses. As it turns out, this doesn't happen very often, but when it does, it can be hard to uncover and may cause serious problems, especially if the defects were to somehow make it through to the market.

The risks are high, and it pays to take every precaution and be as proactive and preemptive as possible.

However, as Reagan would also say, and as a placard on his Oval Office desk read, "It CAN be done."

TAO BY JIMMY: THE WAY INSIDE

Between meetings, we wandered to a nearby coffee shop. Vietnam, the second-largest coffee exporter behind Brazil, delivers the goods when it comes to a quality cup of joe.

Just as we reached the stand, a familiar minivan pulled up beside us. It was our pal, Jimmy. "Hey, are you looking for something?" he asked. I responded, "We're shopping for candles." He smiled and handed me my book on tunnels, lost days earlier. "How did you find this?" I asked, surprised. "You left it in the back," he said. The better question hit me, "How did you find us?" It was peak tourist season, and we were standing in a sea of Western-appearing foreigners in the busiest part of town.

Jimmy's answer was perfectly brilliant. "I'm on the inside," he declared, as if it were the most obvious thing in the world. We laughed and nodded, as if he needed our validation.

Long after the trip, Chad and I would recall Minh and our efforts to pierce the veil of middlemen and get into "candle land." In truth, we had passed through to the inside, a place not typically accessible to foreigners, as we'd be told time and again during our growing business experience in Vietnam.

We wrapped up our inspector meetings with several strong prospects to address further back home.

ART OF THE DA NANG DEAL

It was time for a short flight to Da Nang. Upon arrival, we settled into a Marriott, more convenient for Huy. His factory looked just as we'd left it, complete with the same warm greeting, dogs and tropical-shirt-clad Huy.

This time, though, he had thoroughly prepared. He had our designs ready for review in the showroom and was eager to show improvements made to the wick insertion line, based on our last discussion.

The samples were spot on, with one exception, the glass. We'd tackled the glass issue before, even going so far as to import glass directly, sometimes filling in the U.S. or Mexico. Once again, we saw where we could help, and Huy agreed.

The open topics were price and terms. Price came together fairly easily. We'd need to work out sourcing arrangements for China glass and the logistics flow, but nothing that raised concerns.

Where we hit a snag was on payment terms.

We were reminded of that earlier conversation over pizza, when Huy explained how he'd been burned. Chad and I knew we needed to resolve this. In global sourcing, once your purchase volume hits a certain threshold, best practice is to leverage that scale for extended payment terms, definitely no advance deposits.

There are many levers on the seller's side of the deal, but this one belongs to the buyer.

We went several rounds but hit an impasse. Even the dogs were agitated. That's when Chad tapped into his Harvard business playbook. We were all about to get a lesson in the "cash flow theory of volume."

Chad began sketching out charts, illustrating how our proposed blanket PO, with weekly container releases, would create steady, recurring cash inflow. That inflow, he explained, would buffer risk and spread-out fixed costs. It was a masterclass.

Huy wasn't an easy sell, but eventually we reached a compromise. We'd pay a deposit on the first few containers and he would carry costs for the initial glass supply. Over a short period of time, we'd shift to extended terms with no deposit. He was in. Celebration was in order.

THE REAL EDGE

That wrapped the essentials for the trip. The next morning, we flew back to Saigon to catch our return to LA. As a small reprieve, we connected through Taipei, no lounge issues this time.

I carried the plane,

and everything it represented,

with me the whole way home.

Looking back, the trip was packed with lessons, high points, challenges, and moments of humility. Minh was a good teacher. We learned that the Vietnamese market, though large and layered, isn't a game of hide and seek. Some factories want to be found; they just need help stepping outside their comfort zones.

In global sourcing, you're often the hunter. You watch for patterns, pick up on clues, and trust your instincts. For us, the clue was a pricing structure that didn't add up. Yet spotting a clue is only the beginning, action must follow. Sometimes, there's a person like Minh to lead the way. More often, there's not.

You gather intelligence, dig deeper, and stay persistent.

The path to the "inside" exists,

but it must be pursued with relentless drive.

Taking the time to understand Huy's hesitations from past export experiences was a lesson in itself. Things don't have to start perfect. If there's enough value in the deal and a workable path forward, trust can grow and results blossom over time.

Relationships worth building require mutual investment and sacrifice. Too often, global buyers celebrate "winning" by forcing a deal the supplier can't afford.

In my experience, the factory will eventually claw its way back to a more evenhanded outcome. Remember salt and pepper? Those and more.

This wasn't just another trip. It was a turning point.

We left with more than exceeding pricing targets, we left with leverage, alignment, and clarity on what it takes to win the long game. Relationships, not transactions.

Insight, not assumptions.

Most of all, a reminder that the real edge in global sourcing isn't found on paper.

It's earned on the ground.

2

"YOU'RE IN CHINA NOW": THE PHRASE THAT SAID IT ALL

Midway through what began as a straightforward multinational sourcing trip that started in India, the unexpected found us, when a presidential endorsement for kebobs went terribly wrong, detouring the journey into the unscripted and uncharted. There were bananas, out-of-control rickshaws, and one fateful ferry ride from Hong Kong to Mainland China that led to an armpit incident, a medical quarantine, and brief military custody. Before it was all said and done, we encountered long-toothed monkeys, masquerading monks, calls out to Dexter, a picture book that was won, not purchased, and one solemn cry for the Holiday Inn. Despite the challenges, the full schedule was met, objectives achieved, but not without being tested in ways all too familiar to anyone who's ever lived hands-on sourcing.

With a break over the weekend, my colleague Chris and I decided on a day trip to the Taj Mahal, about a four-hour drive from Delhi. Our hotel helped arrange a taxi to take us there and back.

It was late spring, and the heat was full throttle. The concierge advised us to take some water for the car ride. Agreeing that was a good idea, we loaded in with a full case of those small, hospitality-sized water bottles, the kind you're offered while waiting for your car at the valet. We were confident that overall quantity would adequately compensate for individual volume.

Off we went. It was early, and the sun was rising, masking the transition from city to outskirts at daybreak, and the morning's heat, for that matter.

For those who haven't had the pleasure of driving in India, it can be a shock to the senses. First of all, there's an orchestra of horns that sounds more like language than noise. In the absence of turn signals, checking mirrors, or staying within the lines, what's left are short and long honks that somehow keep traffic in blissful harmony, while appearing and sounding completely chaotic.

For a moment, I thought I was beginning to understand the flow and beeps. A quick double-tap definitely meant, *I'm coming by fast, ready or not.* That seemed to be the most common move. There might have been another half or full tap to signal *I'm on your right* or *left side,* but I couldn't decipher that part with any real certainty. Thankfully, our driver was well-versed in Delhi's chorus of chaos.

The sun was in its full glory by the time we left the city views behind, passing farmland and mustard fields, with the occasional glimpse of distant temples.

Our trip took place before the Yamuna Expressway was fully built, so it was a more rugged journey than it would be today.

That's about when we realized the AC in the car had either tapped out, or was never really working to begin with. It wasn't long after that we had our first interaction with wildlife.

Our driver hit the brakes. The truck next to us swerved. A scooter stopped, then turned around. Traffic slowed to a standstill all around us. There wasn't a sound. It was the stillest any Indian roadway might ever be.

What for, you might ask? *Mother cow.* She had grazed past the roadside and was now more interested in wandering into the traffic lanes than eating. Chewing slowly, ears flicking, she wasn't in a hurry. She didn't need to be. In keeping with India's Hindu roots, the cow is sacred, and at that moment, we were among the reverent.

Eventually, she grew bored with us and moved back out of the way. The moment she cleared the lane, traffic and horns resumed as if someone had hit "play." Our driver was pleased with the interruption. "We are blessed. She looked at us," he said proudly.

Feeling blessed, we were back on our way to Agra. Other than time, the modest cost for this blessing was about four water bottles each, drained in the blistering heat at a standstill. All things considered, we'd clocked enough heat and mileage to justify a turnoff at the next rest stop.

MONKEY BUSINESS

As we returned to the car at the rest stop, our second encounter with wildlife had already arrived, this time in the form of three Rhesus monkeys. Their handlers, dressed in T-shirts and sandals, stood beside our car holding the monkeys up like they were offering entertainment, or a warning.

The monkeys bared their inch-long canine teeth, and we quickly realized we were the latest mark in a well-oiled tourism trap. "Picture... picture with monkey!" Not knowing what else to do, we posed for a photo, and paid the price. Nobody wanted to upset those monkeys. Without rupees on hand, we handed over $5 each, which, judging by the reaction, was more than fair. We jumped back in the car, thinking we were done. We weren't.

Apparently, word traveled fast, and the payment was generous. More handlers and more monkeys began to emerge, surrounding the car. Some of them actually started pushing on the car, thankfully the handlers, not the monkeys, inviting us out for more photo ops.

Our driver gave a three-tap on the horn, surely the universal signal for *move it or lose it*. We pulled away smoothly, leaving the monkey shakedown and simian circus behind. The back seat was full of empty water bottles.

That turned out to be the extent of the adventure before the attraction. We arrived in Agra and reached the Taj Mahal late morning. A guided tour was waiting for us, one that would take us through the site and later shuttle us to a shopping spot, where our driver would reconnect with us for the long haul back to Delhi.

As we approached the Taj, it became immediately clear, that all the pictures I'd seen, those iconic images of the 17th-century monument, featured among the Seven Wonders of the modern world, did not begin to capture its splendor. The mirror-like reflection in the water. The symmetry. The four minarets standing tall around the central dome. The white Makrana marble, glowing in the sunlight. Any one of those elements would be an incredible sight. All-together, it was breathtaking.

SYMMETRY AND SALESMANSHIP

We followed the crowd, placing our shoes among the growing collection gathered near the entrance. Just as we were about to go inside, a young boy, maybe 12, approached, selling picture books of the Taj Mahal.

Dressed in khakis, a button-up shirt, and sandals, he looked just like young Jamal from *Slumdog Millionaire*, which I had seen only days before the trip. With the movie fresh in my mind, his presence tugged at my heart a little more than expected. "Picture book, sir?"

If I'm with family or friends and somehow get separated at a cultural site, museum, or national park, they know exactly where to find me, the gift shop. Easily distracted, I'm usually the one thumbing through books about the tour I'm actively missing, hoping to learn what I should be looking at up close and personal.

Needless to say, a picture book of the Taj was already on my shopping list. This time, though, I wanted to fully experience this stunning testament to an emperor's love, in all its glory, firsthand. I politely told the boy, "Maybe later, after we come back." He didn't flinch. Confidence beaming, he simply said, "No problem, sir. I wait here for you." I hoped he wasn't actually waiting only for me. However, I thought, if he was there when we came back, I'd be more than happy to buy the book from him.

Inside, we saw the cenotaphs, symbolic memorials to both Emperor Shah Jahan and his beloved wife, Mumtaz Mahal, who had inspired the creation of the Taj Mahal as a grand mausoleum in her memory. The messages, both written and visual, depicting paradise and peace, were deeply moving. It is a timeless love story.

After about thirty minutes, we followed our guided group back out to retrieve our shoes and head to the old town shopping spot that came with the tour. I had forgotten about Jamal. He hadn't forgotten about me.

Shoes on, ready to leave, he appeared, smiling, book in hand. He reminded me about the picture book, describing it as the best around. His pitch was well rehearsed and effective. UNESCO World Heritage Site photos… written in English… "All the pictures, you don't need to take any, they are all here," he said proudly.

I was sold. I stepped forward to close the deal. Just as I reached for my wallet, our tour guide waved him off. "No," he said.

"It's not allowed to buy from street vendors." I was surprised, but I followed my internal compass, one that usually says, defer to the rules when abroad, especially if you're not sure what they are.

We climbed aboard an oversized rickshaw, a marvel in its own right, seating about ten people. Just as we started to pull away, something happened that felt straight out of Bollywood. Jamal was running behind us. Stack of books waving in the air.

He was fast enough to keep up. I looked at the guide and said, "If you don't stop the rickshaw, I'm jumping off to get the damn book." He must've seen it in my face. I meant it. I had been respectful and compliant up to that point, but enough was enough.

Exhausted by a buyer and seller's mutual determination to close the deal, on something the guide probably would've earned a commission for at the next stop, he reluctantly gave in. I bought a book for everyone on our tour, which pretty much wiped Jamal's inventory clean. There were smiles all around. Except from our frumpy guide, who muttered, "He'll never see the money anyway."

Off we went to the next stop. I was happy, and still have the book, years later. A reminder of one kid's tenacity to literally chase the deal down.

ALL THE ANIMALS

The next stop turned out to be fun. The rug shop pulled Chris in fast, and he was soon knee-deep in wool and silk rugs, full of Islamic geometry, Persian-influenced floral patterns, and craftsmanship that would hold its own anywhere.

The real entertainment, and a great lesson in humility for any self-proclaimed negotiating mastermind, is trying to haggle with a rug merchant in India. Picture this, tightly bound rugs stacked vertically all around you. You haven't even said what you're looking for, and the merchant is already unrolling six-foot rugs one-handed, laying them side by side, overlapping them like playing cards in a magic trick. "This one is 600 knots." "Look at the rich colors on this one." "This silk is so soft, sir, you'll sleep on it and not your bed." I swear one was claimed to change color in the light.

Chris is the best negotiator I've ever seen, but that day, he met his match. Thankfully, DHL was involved in the transaction, so we weren't hauling rugs back to Delhi ourselves

We made one final stop before heading back, a wood-carving shop. After browsing for a bit, I was drawn to a small elephant, about ten inches long and six inches tall. What caught my eye were the tiny carvings of other animals etched around its body. It didn't take long for the shopkeeper to notice my interest.

"All of the animals, sir," he said confidently. I might've mumbled something like, *"All of them?"* By my count, there was certainly a tiger, a horse, a camel, a cobra, and I'm pretty sure the monkey from that morning made an appearance too. Some majors were missing, in my opinion, but again, best salesmen in the world.

We both walked out with a sandalwood elephant, said to feel like silk, smell like devotion, and apparently host the entire animal kingdom.

Last I heard, whenever Chris manages to find the elephant in his house, he places it somewhere visible, just to see how long it'll take before his wife relocates it someplace out of sight. I imagine the rug merchant's prediction about the "value of peace under feet" was better received. My elephant had a similar destiny.

It was discretely evicted a few times before finally earning permanent residence in my home office, joining other travel trinkets, that mean the world to me and absolutely nobody else.

By the time we caught back up with our driver, we had resupplied on water and were ready for the return trip to our hotel in Delhi. Tomorrow was Monday, the start of another full week of supplier visits and meetings in and around Delhi.

BAZAAR BEHAVIOR

Our mission was to assess the sourcing landscape for wax candles as well as their candle holders crafted in every form from glass and wood to metal and stone.

Traditionally, Delhi, Mumbai, and Bangalore reign as India's powerhouses of wax candle production. Jamshedpur, dubbed "Iron City," boasts a thriving cluster of decorative holders made of steel and brass. Firozabad, the so-called "Glass City," dazzles with its blown glass artistry. Morbi wears the title "Ceramic City," while Uttar Pradesh, home to the majestic Taj Mahal, hosts a dense network of artisans working in wood and natural materials, crafting much more than sandalwood elephants.

For this journey, we made Delhi our home base. A shortlist of promising factories in the region had already been selected for on-site visits. The rest were invited to come to us, parading their wares into a hotel conference room we had cleverly transformed into a working showroom.

It wasn't long before the staff in the business lounge grew intrigued by our operation. With the steady showing of candlelight and craftsmanship, the space had taken on the inviting glow of a boutique bazaar, the catchy ambiance fueling their curiosity.

THE GUT CHECK

One evening that week, we found ourselves at a Five-Star hotel restaurant. There was a large family portrait of Bill, Hillary, and Chelsea Clinton, collectively grinning like they'd just been handed the secret to the sauce. This was undoubtedly intended to offer a warm welcome.

Acknowledging this presidential endorsement, we dug into a platter of BBQ kebabs. Between bites, we debriefed the day, including factories visited, offers made against cost targets, qualification, red flags identified, mapping out the strategy for tomorrow's marathon of meetings.

In global sourcing, there's no pause button. Just dinner, sleep when and where you can, rinse and repeat. Veterans of these trips know the routine well. It's a sunrise to midnight grind, and the only real let down comes in the backseat of a minivan, somewhere on an hours long journey to a remote factory. You shut your eyes not only because you're tired, but because staying awake means watching every terrifying lane change. Notably, the occasional sighting of Pizza Hut and KFC along the way is a welcome reminder that all is not lost.

That next day, the drive was anything but peaceful. A creeping dread settled in as we came to terms with an unsettling truth. The BBQ kebabs from the night before were not fit for a state dinner, but very well made for the *situation room*.

We were now deep into the backroads of India, three hours into the drive. In the words famously attributed to President Clinton himself, "If you live long enough, you'll make mistakes." Last night's mistake was now painfully clear.

On arrival, we made the best of our situation. Fortunately, there were windows of reprieve long enough to tour the factory floor, convene meetings in the showroom to discuss design possibilities, and plan out next steps to see if this supplier might actually be a fit.

PEELING BACK THE LAYERS

That evening, still far from the refuge of our hotel, and farther still from the concept of rest, we were whisked off to a dinner hosted by the factory's management.

It's worth remembering that these sourcing trips don't happen on a whim. They're the result of months of prep, from late-night calls across time zones and date lines, carefully nurtured introductions, rounds of capability reviews, and endless sample evaluations. All that groundwork, just to get to the point where someone says, "Yes, it's worth flying halfway around the world to see it for ourselves."

As is customary on these trips, the days are for business, with quality overviews, production evaluations and design iterations, the nights are for relationship building over copious amounts of food and drink.

These dinners, always graciously hosted by the factory's management, serve two clear purposes. First, to recognize their team's hard work, and second, to create a more relaxed setting where introductions across departments can evolve into working relationships. A little wine goes a long way in supply chain diplomacy.

In American business culture, building relationships often takes a backseat to bottom lines and bullet points. Elsewhere in the world, especially on sourcing trips like this, it's understood that trust is built over shared meals, not spreadsheets.

As we took our seats, visibly hesitant to tempt fate with another meal, the factory owner took a different approach.

Channeling his inner health guru, he launched into a heartfelt sermon on the healing powers of bananas. Potassium packed with electrolyte restoring powers, he proclaimed. He assured us that bananas were the safest bet on the menu.

Somehow, we got through it all and made it back to the hotel for much needed R&R. That was it for the stop in Delhi this time around.

FORMULA ONE... BATHROOM

We moved on from Delhi to Bangalore for the next leg of our candle expedition, with a factory visit set against the unlikely backdrop of a Formula 1 exhibition that had swept through the city and cleared out nearly every hotel room in its path. Of course, we had reserved lodging far in advance, so we thought.

Upon arrival, to our dismay, horror really, a snafu with our reservation had occurred. There weren't two rooms, and no backup options in town. What there was, apparently due to its exorbitant price, was one remaining suite available with a master bedroom and a couch bed in an adjoining room.

We settled into the arrangement, including terms spoken and unspoken. The open and non-negotiable of which being that Chris pulled rank and claimed the only bedroom. I took up residence on the coach, which oddly felt quite comfortable.

Whatever healing powers the bananas once promised had long since expired. Feeling slightly functional, I volunteered to hunt down a local pharmacy. Maybe it was the logistics manager in me, but the idea of another flare up in a suite with one bathroom triggered my inner emergency response protocol.

I obtained directions to a pharmacy from the hotel concierge scribbled onto a notepad that I hoped the taxi driver would understand. It quickly became apparent that no cars were in the neighborhood. I climbed into a motorized rickshaw and sped off into the Bangalore streets. A few bumpy miles later, we pulled up to what looked less like a pharmacy and more like an abandoned warehouse.

Hope springs eternal. I knocked. Surrounded by cardboard and shopping carts turned storage bins, a friendly woman in a white coat greeted me, then flicked on the lights. She listened patiently to my story.

I probably overexplained the situation. Without hesitation and all business, she pointed to a metal ladder leading to a dimly lit mezzanine loft area, and instructed me to help myself to a few items. She rattled off their names, each sounding like the full scientific identity of what I assumed *Imodium* must be. I was on the hunt for "Loperamide hydrochloride."

A bushel of bananas in, it somehow felt fitting to go climbing through what could only be described as a pharmacy turned jungle, with shelves stacked to the rafters, unlabeled baskets with mixed products, boxes crammed into crevices, font types on the packaging equivalent to fine printed legal copy that would make any attorney proud. Against the odds, the scavenger hunt was a success. I located the goods, bought out their entire supply, and climbed back down from the ladder feeling triumphant.

I hopped back into the rickshaw. Medicine secured and feeling embolden, I made the mistake of mentioning the race in town. Turns out, my driver was a fan of the nearby F1 exhibition, and he decided this was the perfect time to showcase what his vehicle could really do. The ride back morphed into something between a carnival ride and the Monaco Grand Prix.

He literally rolled up a curb, popped a wheelie, and took sidewalk shortcuts. I had apparently hailed Bangalore's number one motorsport enthusiast with a rickshaw license. The good news? I made it back to tell this story

WAX SCENE INVESTIGATION (WSI)

By the next morning, the meds had finally kicked in, and we were ready to see what Bangalore had to offer.

Often referred to as India's Silicon Valley, the city had a noticeably more relaxed energy than Delhi. The climate, cooler and breezier, was a welcome relief from the intense heat we'd just escaped. We had only one factory visit planned, a candle manufacturer that came highly recommended. A car had been arranged to pick us up. The drive wasn't far, maybe eight miles, to a well-established industrial park just beyond the city's edge.

Along the way, we passed through a sprawling transit hub called Majestic, more urban theater than bus depot. At one point, we had to dodge a swarm of buses moving with improvised precision, like a choreographed stampede.

Not long after, we arrived. The factory, from the outside, was a modest concrete structure, weathered, but still holding its own. We entered through a corrugated metal gate that no longer seemed capable of closing all the way. Immediately noticeable was a tangled mass of exposed electrical wiring clinging to one side of the building like an external nervous system.

As we parked, our contact, Deepak, stepped out to greet us, joined by a few team members in uniform. After some quick pleasantries, we made our way inside. The conference room, doubling as a showroom, featured a lineup of candles ranging in shape, size, and function.

The display suggested a reasonably competent operation. We were cautiously optimistic.

The tour began. A few unorthodox production methods surfaced here and there, but nothing disqualifying, until we reached the wax processing room. What we saw next was unlike anything we'd encountered.

Red and white wax sprayed from a machine into large hopper carts, or was supposed to. Much of it missed entirely. A shocking amount had hit the walls and ceiling, splattering upward in such volume that it had begun to form stalactite-like drips, hardened into streaks over time. The red wax, in particular, gave the whole mess a crime-scene vibe.

I wasn't sure whether to alert *Dexter* for splatter analysis, *Elvira* for a classic horror assessment, or *Bill Nye* to understand the science behind what we were witnessing. I decided to turn to Deepak, who couldn't rationally explain either but said, "everything is ok."

It's always unfortunate when something goes sideways early in a visit. While it was already clear this wouldn't be a fit, professional courtesy, and basic decency, meant we'd see it through politely.

We stayed a bit longer, wrapped up the visit with a respectful exit, and headed back to the hotel, with bags to pack, China up next.

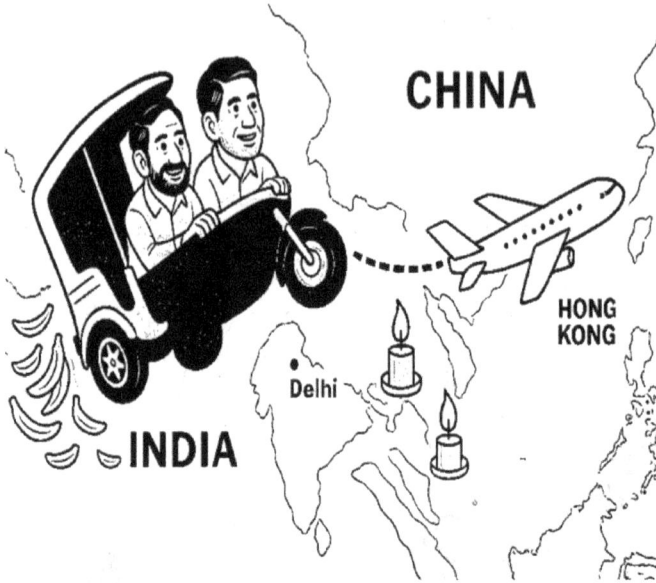

EVE OF DISRUPTION

We were heading to Mainland China, by way of Hong Kong. More precisely, to the city of Zhuhai in Guangdong province. The mission was shifting, too, moving beyond candles and decorative devices into the world of portable household appliances and early concepts for an emerging outdoor retail camping line.

When doing business in China, Hong Kong is a smart place to start as a logistics base of operation. From there, you can fan out on regional flights to key Mainland cities, crisscrossing supply areas, before circling back to Hong Kong for the longer haul home. What's more, Hong Kong has a way of offering weary travelers from abroad a taste of home.

Nowhere is that more apparent than in *Lan Kwai Fong*, or "LKF" if you'd like to sound like you've been there before. It's a compact, energetic pocket of the city where you can bounce from an Australian steakhouse to a tiki bar, slip into a hookah lounge, catch some live music, and soak in a vibrant atmosphere.

Getting there is easy enough, about a 40-minute drive from the international airport to Central on Hong Kong Island, with a quick zip through the underwater Cross-Harbor Tunnel.

A word of caution for the uninitiated. After dark, especially in the late-night hours, what appear to be Buddhist monks may approach with beaded bracelets, an offer of prayer, and hopeful eyes. They're probably not monks. They're likely hustlers in robes, swapping trinkets for "donations." As the saying goes, "nothing good happens after midnight."

In LKF, your grandmother's advice was never more relevant. Best to enjoy a stellar dinner, take in the electric pulse of the scene, and head back for a decent night's rest before duty calls for the next leg of the journey. That alarm will sound earlier than you realize. The ferry will leave without you... in the rush, you'll forget something like your passport... And, grandma's wisdom applies well wherever you are.

Feeling renewed, this time, we did make an overnight stop in Lan Kwai Fang, and met up with a former supplier who had become a close friend to us both.

A treat awaited, an Italian feast, full of risotto, bruschetta, and tiramisu. French-born and at that point longtime expat based in Hong Kong, he was a generous host and we were grateful. The conversation hit topics from politics to culture to sports, and of course touched on business. The wine poured and night went long in good company. Of course, we were in bed before midnight, or that's how I remember it. I guess my credibility is questionable if I am telling stories of late-night masquerading monks.

For my travel partner and I, it was a relief to have our appetites back, thanks to bananas, familiar meds found abroad, and some time for it all to work itself out.

There's a point in every international business trip, usually somewhere midway, when the body has fully acclimated and there's the right fusion of atmosphere and business cadence. It's usually something different each time. If you're lucky, it happens more than once. At this point, speaking for myself, it was this Italian dinner.

Back at my room, I thought, so far so good, a couple bumps in the road notwithstanding. We had a long time left on this trip and little did I know then of what's to come.

The next day would prove the opposite of that coveted day of awesomeness. One extreme bear another. Not as predictable or even as frequent, the one calamity, hopefully only one, during the trip, also rears its ugly head.

In this regard, I had a date with destiny. It would be tomorrow where I would have an adventure all my own.

ARMPIT INCIDENT

It was an early rise the next morning, and with passports in hand and a bit more spring in our step, we made our way to the ferry station. We were ready for whatever the next stop had in store, or so we thought.

Since 2018, Hong Kong and Zhuhai have been linked by a sweeping feat of engineering, a bridge-highway and undersea tunnel system touted as the world's longest sea crossing. Before that, during the time of this trip, the go-to route was a far more modest affair in the form of an hour-long ferry ride across the Pearl River Delta.

Earlier in the week, local news reports had sounded the alarm about one confirmed case of H1N1, Swine Flu, having surfaced in the area. The individual had flown from the U.S. to Hong Kong International Airport, entering Mainland China via ferry terminal through Macau. At the time, Zhuhai's population hovered around 1.3 million, while the broader Guangdong province Zhuhai belonged to, boasted over 83 million residents.

At those numbers, even a single case was enough to raise serious concerns that the situation could quickly spread. It wouldn't be long until local authorities would encounter another suspected positive case of Swine Flu, coming in on a ferry from Hong Kong.

If you haven't figured it out yet, your final clue is that the suspect is no stranger to bananas and would cry foul to any Yelp review associated with the former first family during the '90's.

As our ferry approached Jiuzhou Port in Zhuhai, an announcement crackled over the loudspeakers, first in Chinese, then in English, instructing all passengers to cooperate with Chinese medical personnel who would soon be boarding.

Minutes later, a small brigade of about eight in white coats descended onto the deck and below, each wielding a handheld infrared thermometer.

Feeling much better, but knowing I still had a slight fever, I couldn't help but feel anxious.

Sometimes "it's better to be lucky than good" as the saying goes. When my turn came it was a quick forehead brush with success. No problem, passed the screening… *"Break on through to the other side"* was the song lyric that played in my head.

It wasn't long before Little Richard's, *"Keep a-knockin' but you can't come in"* played next.

Before my eyes, was the ominous sight of a row of tables, each with a cup of thermometers and much larger crew of white coats. This line of defense also included Chinese soldiers, carrying rifles, composed and ready.

My colleague and I took our seats at one of the inspection tables. I went first, reaching into the cup to grab a thermometer. Instinct took over and I brought it straight to my mouth, because, well, that's what you do, right? Evidently, we never stop learning.

If I'd hoped to fly under the radar, that plan unraveled fast. My colleague, and at least two other ferry passengers, immediately shouted and gestured for me to *STOP!* This attracted the attention of several nearby nurses, who now turned toward me with a mix of concern and curiosity. Before I could make a bigger scene, the well-meaning Good Samaritans clarified, somewhat urgently, that the thermometer was meant to go under my arm, not in my mouth.

Whatever my body temperature was when I stepped off the ferry, it had surely climbed a few degrees by now. Sweat was running down my forehead as I awkwardly and gingerly tried to wedge the thermometer under my arm. The intent was compliance but perhaps with less zeal than expected.

My subtle maneuver caught the attention of the obvious nurse in charge. Her physique matched her apparent authority.

With broad shoulders turned toward me, eyes locked on with surgical precision, she marched over deliberately. Without a word, she drove the thermometer deep into my armpit. The next song playing in my mental jukebox? *"I fought the law, and the law won."*

What unfolded next was the kind of moment that makes you look for hidden cameras.

One of the soldiers gently guided my colleague toward the immigration line. The last I heard from him was his voice from the other side of the terminal, over the ruckus of the crowd. A desperate cry reached me, "What is our hotel?" I turned back for just a moment, the distance between us growing as he continued to be ushered ahead and I was stuck in place. I shouted with all the clarity I could muster, "Holiday Inn!" Then he was gone.

As for me, things escalated, fast. The head nurse was true to form, assuming role of playmaker. A huddle formed with a team of fellow nurses, then a soldier was waved over. The call had been made. In no uncertain terms, access was denied to this foreigner. What seemed like a brilliant idea came to mind.

"Can I just take the ferry back to Hong Kong?" I asked, somewhat desperately. The reply was perfectly clear and left no room for misunderstanding. *"No, you're in China now!"*

That would be the last English I'd hear for the next twelve hours. Inside the ambulance, my final *lifeline* I thought would be *Phone a friend*. I called back to the office and I quickly summarized the situation. The call ended with my question about whether legal representation should be pursued on my behalf, which was meant to be serious not funny.

Another not-so-brilliant idea, to think about American notions of constitutional law in communist China while in military custody. In response, "Thanks for letting us know… keep us posted." Less than confidence building, I thought. Though I found out later, my colleague had already called and they were in fact working to engage capable counsel, and our supplier that we had plans to visit that next day was also notified, ready to assist in any way possible.

However, it was clear to all, including myself, nothing could be done until it was settled as to whether or not I actually had the Swine Flu. I started to second guess the food poisoning theory. What if I did have the Swine Flu, I thought. Truth be told, I didn't even know what Swine Flu was!

CLEARED FOR ENTRY

It didn't take long to reach the Hospital; a towering structure pressed against a hillside bursting with wildflowers. As the ambulance door opened, I was met by a man who appeared to be a doctor.

He greeted me with a mix of Mandarin and purposeful hand gestures universally communicating, *follow me*. We took an elevator up a few floors, walked down a brightly lit hallway, and entered a private hospital room with one bed. It wasn't the Holiday Inn, but my sense was this would be my lodging for tonight.

The Doctor left, and another man walked in with a lighter colored uniform. He waved me over to follow him. We went back down the elevator to the ground level and exited the building. Then, he jumped on a bicycle and peddled about 50 yards ahead, while I trailed behind on foot, stopping every few minutes for me to catch up.

We finally made it to another building, which led to a radiology room, revealed by the universal radiation symbol. A chest X-ray followed.

Then, we retraced our way back, my footsteps, his tire tracks, to my original waiting room.

About an hour later, a female nurse entered. A cup of noodles in hand, and a needle concealed until minutes later. It was time to have my blood drawn, then, apparently, dinner.

More time passed, before the phone rang inside the room. Who could be calling me? Who even knows I am here? Out of either boredom or curiosity, I picked up and despite all that'd transpired felt playful enough to answer in Chinese… "Ni Hao" I said.

In reply, to my surprise, was… "hello sir, this is the United States Center for Disease Control." "I need to ask you a few questions." There may have been something along the lines of, "how are you feeling" but if so, it wasn't the memorable part of the conversation.

I said, "sure, ask away." The Q&A went into the basics about when I first experienced symptoms, prior countries visited. On the other end of the phone, the greatest point of interest came from who I was traveling with, sat next to on the flight into Hong Kong, where and what I had done leading up to that fateful ferry ride. I provided a detailed account, weaving in references to monks and tiramisu.

The nurse returned, as if saving the best for last, pulling one more trick from her sleeve, a long cotton swab for a throat culture. By now, it was getting late, around midnight. I'd been at the hospital for over ten hours. Some more time passed, and then the phone in the room rang again. On the other end was finally a familiar voice, it was Jamie, from the factory we were scheduled to visit the next day.

I'd always wondered how effective the Chinese visa process really was. For business travelers, China's visa requires an invitation letter from a Chinese company, effectively making them your host and raising their level of responsibility. Apparently, contact had been made with my host, because Jamie was now on the phone.

She had good news, the blood test, chest x-ray, and throat culture all came back negative for Swine Flu. They were on their way to pick me up.

While I waited, there was one final surprise, a parting gift. The nurse with the needle returned. This time, I'd be on the receiving end. Did I know what I was about to be injected with? Absolutely not. Still only Mandarin on this side of the landline. Oddly enough, I didn't protest. I blindly trusted it was in my best interest, or subconsciously figured my objection would be overruled. The whole ordeal had been exhausting. The shot was over quickly, and Jamie arrived shortly after. I was free to go.

On to the Holiday Inn we went. At the front desk, I handed over my passport to check in and casually mentioned that I'd been held up a bit on arrival. The friendly attendant smiled and said, "We know all about it. We were notified of the good news that you passed the medical exam."

I asked about my colleague, wanting to make sure he'd arrived safely, thinking back to how abrupt our separation had been at the ferry terminal nearly twelve hours earlier. She nodded and said, "Yes, he's here," then added that they'd been standing by, waiting to hear how my test results turned out.

Had I tested positive, she explained, the authorities would've been by to collect him next, for his turn to chase the bicycle over to radiology, symptoms or not.

HOT UNDER THE COLLAR

After some of the best sleep I'd ever had, it was time to keep our original appointment the next morning with Jamie and her team. The plan was to discuss a design change to an existing food preparation device and review a few new camping items.

Thankfully, the meeting would be held in the hotel's business lounge, with all prototypes and specifications ready for review.

Chris and I met over breakfast before heading to the lounge and had a good laugh recounting the ordeal at the ferry terminal. We were officially back on track.

Still, something felt different. I didn't just feel better. I felt incredible. Rejuvenated. Energized. Then I noticed it.

My shirt was soaked, and sweat was dripping from my hair and brow. Whatever mystery cocktail I'd been injected with at the hospital was clearly kicking in.

Refreshed and light on my feet, I walked into the room, hand out, eager to greet the team and dive into the work. I could sense a bit of trepidation from our factory partners, but they played along. After all, I'd been cleared for entry. Whether it was an antiviral, a vitamin boost, or something else entirely, the shot had done the trick.

STRONGER TOGETHER

We stayed on schedule the next several days, visiting suppliers across China before catching our return flight home to Los Angeles. I'd left in good form and, miraculously, returned the same.

Everything in between? Chalk it up to another sourcing adventure, the kind that never makes it into the job description, either because it's too unpredictable, or it would scare people off.

Chris and I bonded on this trip in a way only these types of experiences can mold. We'd return for many more over the years, thankfully less eventful but no less fruitful. That's the thing, there's real value in having a teammate with chemistry and complementary skills. Sourcing trips aren't just about factories and forecasts. They're about long-haul flights, shared cars, random detours, and the occasional digestive crisis. Fourteen-hour days. Sleepless nights. You learn a lot about a person in those moments.

When you've got the right team, those shared struggles become building blocks. The work gets sharper, the collaboration tighter, and the chances of success go way up. When it all comes together and things are clicking, that same team will catch what others miss.

That's when the magic happens.

3

DESERT TERMS:
WHAT THE SAND DIDN'T SAY

Newly promoted and dangerously optimistic, I boarded a flight to Saudi Arabia, more Jason Bourne than global buyer, with a pitch deck in one hand and a second passport in the other. I came for a fuel deal… and found myself off the grid in the desert badlands, crossing paths with locals who knew more about why I shouldn't be there but were impressed that I was. Before it was over, the journey would involve one boardroom, one camel, one bead shop, one bonfire, and an infinite amount of hope under the stars. From the moment it began, it was clear, this was no ordinary sourcing trip. Years later, long after plans were overtaken by events in the region, a pearl of wisdom was unearthed, teaching that harvests take time and what grows may be a different form than expected…but taste even more delicious.

Author's Chapter Note:

As a preamble to this story, some moments are shared with a dose of humor, mostly at my own expense. While there's room for levity in the details of my experience, I've made every effort to approach the broader events with the respect they deserve. There is no intent to make light of the serious realities or atrocities tied to this time of war. Any humor reflects my own missteps, misunderstandings, and lessons learned in unfamiliar settings.

BOURNE-READY IN THE DESERT

A business visit to Saudi Arabia was no small task in early 2003. Once I received the formal invitation letter from the petrochemical company I planned to visit, I applied in person at the Saudi Consulate in Los Angeles. I also had sourcing interests for ambiance products manufactured in Israel, which could involve a future visit.

Under the Kingdom's entry rules, a prior visit to Israel, visible as a passport stamp, could result in being denied entry to Saudi Arabia. To avoid any conflicts, I applied for a second U.S. passport specifically for future Israel travel.

Aside from navigating diplomatic sensitivities, having two passports turned out to be an astute play. It's a useful trade maneuver if you're in one country but need to apply for a visa to visit another. For instance, say you're traveling through China with plans to visit Vietnam, and then unexpectedly get an invite to a factory in Korea. With two passports, you can send one off for Korean visa processing while continuing travel with the other, both endorsed and ready for their respective countries when you need them. Some countries offer visas on arrival, but many still require in advance. In any case, it's more efficient to avoid the delay of applying in person upon arrival.

Passports in hand, I had officially leveled up as a global business traveler. I now joined the ranks of those armed with more than one passport, sure to make for great conversation at business dinners.

Eventually, my Saudi visa was approved. It came adorned with the Kingdom's emblem of crossed swords and a palm tree, and most notably, several postage-stamp-style endorsements that gave it an old-world gravitas. A fitting credential for the exciting journey ahead.

The timing of the trip couldn't have been more pivotal in my young career.

I was 31, recently promoted, now overseeing, among other areas, the full scope of supply chain and sourcing. Our company operated in institutional and consumer products, with most manufactured domestically across company factories. Several of our core products relied on petrochemical-based fuels, some of which were broadly available, others more specialized.

One of those specialty fuels, a byproduct not widely used in other industries, happened to be one we consumed in large volume. As an attractive reality, that very compound was produced in abundance by a subsidiary of Saudi Arabia's national oil company. Not only was their supply steady, but their production costs were among the lowest in the world, and their capacity was more than sufficient to meet our growing needs for the foreseeable future, even accounting for ambitious expansion plans.

The objective was to explore the feasibility of building a factory in Saudi Arabia to fill and package the chemical into canisters for direct export to the U.S. as finished goods, an operation that would be supplied directly by the Saudi chemical company. Discussions around manufacturing in Saudi began as early as 2000. For obvious reasons, the project was shelved in the wake of September 11, 2001.

In early 2003, we decided to revisit the opportunity. A Saudi-based investor was already onboard, and an American business partner with roots in the region had been brokering the early stages of the deal. The investor had the relationship with the chemical company; the broker had the relationship with the investor. I was chosen to fly over and meet the key players face-to-face. The broker would join me upon my arrival in Dammam and serve as both translator and protector, my escort throughout every step of the journey.

The itinerary was tightly packed, with supplier visits in Dammam, a high-stakes presentation to the chemical division of the royal oil company, and finally, a visit to Al-Hofuf, the proposed site for the factory itself.

Allow me to set the stage. In the spring of 2003, the world was still reeling in the aftermath of 9/11. The War on Terror was fully underway, and global tensions were high. Across the Middle East, atrocities carried out by al-Qaeda and affiliated groups were surfacing with disturbing frequency. According to U.S. State Department records, there were 198 international terrorist attacks recorded in 2002 alone.

At the same time the War on Terror was unfolding, tensions were escalating rapidly between the U.S. and Saddam Hussein's Iraq. A U.S.-led coalition invasion seemed not only likely but increasingly imminent.

In early March 2003, just a week before my departure, momentum toward an Iraq invasion hit a brief snag. The Turkish legislature, under mounting public pressure, voted to deny U.S. forces the use of its territory as a staging ground for any northern offensive, leaving only Kuwait on board in the south.

Days later, an emergency Islamic summit convened in Doha, Qatar, with delegates from more than 50 countries seeking a diplomatic solution to avoid war.

Tensions flared quickly. At one point, a high-ranking Iraqi official offended Kuwait's spokesperson, an exchange that, unsurprisingly, signaled the summit was not going well.

CAMOUFLAGE WELCOME

The following week, I boarded my Lufthansa flight out of LAX, bound first for a connection in Frankfurt. PowerPoint presentation packed, portable projector in tow, I was off. On my first real mission as a young executive, determined to bring back treasure from foreign lands.

I carried the confidence of *Jason Bourne*, paired with the naïveté of a 31-year-old who had never been to the Middle East, about to step, quite literally, into a region on the brink of war.

Even before reaching Saudi, the signs that this wasn't an ordinary business trip began to show. On my connecting flight from Frankfurt to Kuwait City, I quickly noticed that most of the passengers around me were in military camouflage. Turns out, I was sharing a flight with the early wave of what would soon be labeled the "coalition of the willing," deployed to disarm Iraq.

The flight was full, about 200 passengers by my count. I was seated near the back of the Boeing aircraft. Upon landing in Kuwait, an announcement was made instructing those continuing on to Dammam to remain onboard while others deplaned. No surprise who went and who stayed. A sea of camouflage filed out, leaving behind about ten of us in comfortable business-casual attire, all wordlessly exchanging glances that said, *well, here we go.*

Soon after, we lifted off again for the short hop, roughly one hour, to Dammam.

By the time we landed, it was late. Even to a rookie globe-trotter like me, things felt unusual. Our small group, still wearing that shared expression of disbelief, shuffled into the immigration area. There were a dozen inspection lanes, in the brightly lit hall, each manned by an officer, but barely enough passengers to fill one. Processing didn't take long, and soon we were through the check-point and stepping into the sights, sounds, and pulse of the city.

Dammam sits on the eastern coast of Saudi Arabia, along the Persian Gulf, or the Arabian Gulf, depending on which map you choose or politics you observe. For geographic context, Iran lies just across the water. Iraq borders Saudi to the North. Nearby is Ghawar, the world's largest conventional oil field, and the heart of Saudi Arabia's energy dominance.

As a chemical buyer, I was certainly in the right place. Whether it was the right time was still very much up for debate. Waiting outside the airport was my protector-in-chief, the previously mentioned broker named Bassel. It was a short drive to the Sheraton, where I spent the night.

BOXES CHECKED

By sunrise, we were on the move, hitting five supplier visits that day, ranging from can manufacturers to corrugated box makers and wick assembly fabricators.

The pace was fast, the purpose clear. Figure out who could help us make this project real. The factories turned out to be impressive, automated, efficient, and well managed. So far, many of the right boxes were being checked. As I walked the production floors, I noticed familiar logos from Fortune 500 brands back in the States. It was clear that the groundwork to bring these suppliers up to U.S. standards had been laid long ago.

One consistent theme stood out, each facility was primarily operated by a migrant labor force, overseen by Saudi management.

WORRY BEADS AND WARNING SIGNS

The next leg of the trip took us to Riyadh, where we'd go from the factory floor to the boardroom.

While our company wasn't small, in the context of this meeting, our *well* intentions were modest compared to the kingdom's vast resources.

Before the high-stakes part of the trip began, there was still a night in Dammam to enjoy, and Bassel was proving to be good company. We'd already started to bond over the day's events, beginning with an unintentional moment of humility at breakfast. I took the final sip of my Turkish coffee, inexperienced and unaware of the sludge of grounds waiting at the bottom. Choking slightly on the gritty surprise, I looked up to see Bassel laughing. Judging by the look on his face, we'd be friends soon enough.

Bassel was no rookie. He had real roots in the region and close friends in the area. That evening, I'd meet one of them.

Though originally from Syria, Bassel had lived in the states for years. He told me that whenever he was back in Saudi, he never passed up the chance to shop for Islamic prayer beads, what he called, for my benefit, "worry beads." He had a favorite shop in mind. From the way he said it, I could tell this wasn't just a shopping trip. It was a calling.

Bassel had arranged a car and driver to pick us up at the Sheraton. After about 20 minutes on the road, we pulled into an area that looked more like a row of storage units than a retail destination. One nondescript roll-up door stood out. Bassel knocked twice and, like a scene straight out of *Ali Baba and the Forty Thieves*, up it went. Was this the path to stolen treasure? I hoped not. Inside stood a tall, slender man in his forties, coincidentally named Ali, smiling wide as he greeted an old friend.

Ali wasted no time. He popped open a few metal suitcases; each filled with rows of ornate prayer beads. It didn't take long to realize Bassel was not only a seasoned traveler but a talker, especially when it came to politics.

As the two of them boasted about American leadership, I forgot the geopolitical tension brewing just beyond the casual banter. Then Ali gestured toward a calendar on the wall.

March 11 was circled.

"This," he said, "is when the Americans are coming."

He didn't seem like the most credible source, but the timing gave me pause. It was March 9, and we still had four more days in the country. "Not to worry," Bassel said cheerfully. "If anything happens, I can get us to Damascus through Jordan, by car, in less than 24 hours." He said it like it was a perfectly reasonable plan.

Then came that same infectious laugh I'd heard over breakfast with the Turkish coffee grounds. I laughed, too, but mine was noticeably more reserved.

Bassel eventually settled on two sets of beads, one amber, the other onyx. He was absolutely thrilled with the purchase. Ali then turned to me and opened another case, not beads this time. Inside were luxury watches, all slightly used but confidently presented as authentic. At this point, I was seriously starting to wonder if we *had* stumbled onto the ill-gotten bounty of the *Forty Thieves*.

Naturally, Ali offered me a deal on a vintage-looking TAG Heuer that was too good to resist.

AUDIENCE WITH THE KINGDOM

The next morning, we left early for our one-hour flight to Riyadh, the capital of Saudi Arabia.

At first sight, the city is striking, with a skyline of boldly sculpted, futuristic skyscrapers rising from the desert floor, juxtaposed against a horizon that feels eternal. This was a land shaped by prophets, poets, and warriors, now transformed by the modern wealth drawn from what lies beneath.

It was time to suit up. I pulled out the tie, shined my shoes, and prepared for what felt like the first prime-time moment of my young career.

The company we were about to meet wasn't just any regional player. It was the kind of entity routinely visited by world leaders, foreign dignitaries, and the global titans of oil and gas. We weren't aiming to run with that crowd. We just wanted to stay under the radar and be taken seriously enough to earn advantageous pricing for our modest "tail of the dog" chemical and the small factory we hoped to build in Al-Hofuf.

The meeting room was grand, a large, formal conference space anchored by an elegantly crafted mahogany table that seated ten on each side. My first thought was there were more people in the room than passengers on my flight to Dammam.

Bassel and Omar kicked things off with polite conversation, mixing Arabic with just enough English to keep me looped in when it mattered.

It took about twenty minutes for everyone to settle into their seats. The room finally settled, and eyes began turning toward me. I'd used the lead-up to plug in the projector and queue up the Power Point. I was ready. They were ready. From that point forward, English became the primary language, with only the occasional Arabic sidebar.

After brief introductions around the table, the executive in charge, a man named Tariq, set the tone with a surprisingly personal opening remark. "You must be very serious about this business to be here right now," he said, looking directly at me. "Thank you," I replied. "Yes, and it's my pleasure." He gave a small, approving nod. Then, the floor was mine.

The presentation wasn't as interactive as I'd hoped, but I walked through the essentials, our company background, the industries we served, the specific products tied to their chemicals, and the vision for a Saudi-based operation.

Not surprisingly, the bulk of the questions focused on the proposed factory, its investment size, scope, labor plans, and management structure. Many of these questions, I assumed, were already answered in prior discussions that had helped secure the meeting. Nonetheless, it seemed some in the room still wanted to hear it firsthand, to make sure intentions were consistent and clear.

The conversation carried on for about an hour beyond our scheduled time, which I took as a good sign. As we wrapped up, we mentioned that our next stop would be Al-Hofuf to visit the proposed factory site.

As I packed up my materials and others began filing out, Tariq approached me.

"Good presentation," he said.

"We appreciate you coming all this way. We look forward to seeing where it leads. Safe journey."

We'd save the debrief for later. At that moment, it felt like the meeting had gone well.

OFF THE GRID IN THE BADLANDS

It was March 11, and Ali's circled calendar, the cryptic "they're coming" prediction, came back to mind as I waited in the hotel lobby for Bassel.

Omar would be joining us that day. We were headed to Al-Hofuf, the proposed site for the new factory. Omar, an influential investor in the city, would be leading the day's adventure.

Upon Omar's arrival, there was a change in plan. Bassel jumped into Omar's shiny black Suburban for what seemed like the need for a private conversation. I was directed to follow in a separate cab that Bassel had arranged. My ride? An aging Toyota Camry, proudly displaying years of dings and scrapes from loyal service on the desert roadways.

The drive to Al-Hofuf would take over three hours. My driver didn't speak a word of English.

The first 30 minutes took us past logistics hubs and warehouse clusters on Riyadh's outskirts. Soon the skyline faded, replaced by the open stretch of the Najd Plateau. Flat, vast desert surrounded us, interrupted only by the occasional herd of camels in the distance.

The journey was tolerable, temperatures in the mid-80s Fahrenheit, no air conditioning, and sun pouring in through the windows. Still, the Suburban remained in view ahead, kicking up a trail of dust we could follow.

Until it wasn't.

At some point, I'd looked down to review notes from the trip, briefly distracted. When I glanced up again, the Suburban had vanished. Moments later, we exited the highway and continued down a side road for several more miles, eventually arriving at a small roadside village. I checked my BlackBerry and no signal.

I gestured to the driver, and he pointed toward the gas station, momentarily reassuring me that this was just a routine fuel stop after more than two hours on the road.

As we idled, I glanced around and caught a glimpse of my reflection in the window, young-looking, fair-skinned, dressed in Western-style business attire. To anyone outside, I clearly looked European… or American.

As mentioned, it was March 11, 2003. Sporadic terrorist kidnappings had been on the rise in the region. According to Ali, coalition forces might be invading Iraq any day now, possibly to-day. I couldn't help but think, maybe I should've bought the worry beads instead of that watch.

As the driver pumped gas, calmly, casually, there were no obvious red flags. Still, my eyes scanned the area. Faded tire service signs, sun-worn buildings, and rows of rusted metal storefronts gave the impression of a place built to be passed by, not lingered in. Yet, no sign of Bassel or Omar. Where were they?

Soon enough, we were fueled up and back on the road, then onto the highway. I stayed extra vigilant, though a growing sense of helplessness persisted.

About an hour later, we literally entered an oasis, the Al-Ahsa Oasis, to be precise. The desert gave way to clusters of date palms that first appeared like mirages, then quickly multiplied into vast groves.

Our tour of Saudi had started at the Gulf Coast, passed through a glittering metropolis, crossed the barren expanse of the Najd Plateau, and now one of the largest natural oases on Earth.

A short while later, we pulled into the driveway of our destination, a high-rise hotel owned by Omar. Relief washed over me. My stress dropped, spirits lifted, especially when I saw Omar's black Suburban parked just ahead.

The reunion was short-lived, though, as Bassel came flying out of the vehicle like a man unhinged. He stormed toward my driver, launching into a tirade. The words were in Arabic, but the tone needed no translation. Bassel was charged with the raw panic of someone who feared something had gone terribly wrong.

Omar waved him off and approached me with an apology for the separation. Clearly, Bassel's reaction said it all. He had genuinely feared for my safety. The tension I'd been brushing off was very real to him. It was a sobering thought.

That said, no harm done. As promised, we were headed for lunch, which Bassel had confidently billed as the highlight of the trip. A feast had been prepared.

WHERE DEALS ARE SEASONED

This was my first real exposure to the kind of hospitality that often accompanies international business travel, though over the years, my appreciation for it would deepen considerably.

When you're a guest of a local host, you are truly honored. It's not just politeness, it's a cultural code, a way of doing business rooted in traditions that stretch back centuries. More than that, it's a gesture of national pride, a sense of responsibility to represent one's country with dignity, generosity, and warmth, as if serving in the role of cultural ambassador. As a visitor, your response matters. That means approaching the experience with deep respect and sincere gratitude. It might mean trying unfamiliar foods, or simply deferring to the host's lead. There's a certain grace and feel to how meals and social outings complement the more formal moments in offices and factory tours.

The truth I learned early is the decision you're hoping for often isn't made in the meeting room. It's made over tea, during dinner, or on a walk to the car.

One of my personal mantras has always been, *people do business with people.* At a distance, it may look like companies negotiating with companies, but that's an illusion. Interpersonal relationships drive results. Years later, a CEO at a major Chinese oil company told me they had turned down deals with some of the world's largest corporations simply because the representative was arrogant or difficult.

It pays to make the extra effort. Think of it like a first date. Or a dream job interview. And, *always*, treat the meal like something your mom cooked. If you bring that mindset, you'll be well on your way to living out Dale Carnegie's call to *win friends and influence people*, no matter the country.

The feast was served in a private banquet hall on the top floor of the hotel. It would be just the three of us, Bassel, Omar, and myself.

The meal was served family style, as is tradition. We shared grilled *Hamour*, fragrant *Basmati* rice with lamb, chicken *Kabsa*, and warm, fresh *Khubz Tannour* flatbread. I followed the lead of Omar and Bassel and ate with my hands, something that takes a bit of getting used to. A couple points of etiquette stood out, use only your right hand, and eat only from the area of food directly in front of you. Bonus points for mastering the three-finger method of thumb, index, and middle.

As we ate, the conversation shifted naturally to the previous day's meeting with the chemical company. Both Bassel and Omar were pleased with the feedback they'd received. Full support, they reported. I asked if the pricing looked favorable. Bassel smiled and told me it would be even better than projected.

That explained the need for the private setting in the Suburban. Turns out, the two of them had used the morning to hash out capital structure, construction plans, equipment needs, and early labor considerations. However, their focus on the road ahead had left me behind, in the rearview.

JOB OFFER I COULD REFUSE

We headed out to see the proposed site. It was a modest industrial park, but strategically located, just a stone's throw from the chemical plant that would supply the fuel, and close enough to other key materials and packaging vendors. Finished goods would be exported through Dammam Port, roughly 80 miles away.

Eventually, the facility would need a Managing Director. Both Bassel and Omar asked what I thought about taking on the role. "Thank you," I said, "but that's a bridge too far for me." I suggested a couple of candidates who I felt would be better suited for the job. They listened and nodded, then casually described the kind of lifestyle the position would offer.

The future plant manager would live in a residential compound, a gated community of villas with an international school and every amenity imaginable, including swimming pool, restaurants, a bowling alley, gym, and more.

Bassel, ever the salesman, added that there would even be a weekend travel stipend to Bahrain, a nearby island in the Gulf, known for being far more liberal than Saudi Arabia. On the island, alcohol was served in bars and restaurants, and tastes of Western culture and entertainment was readily available. Though it closed in 2019, at the time, there was even a Hard Rock Café in Bahrain, the kind of comforting landmark that signals to American business travelers they're not *that* far from home... or mozzarella sticks. Bahrain, he noted, was just under two hours away by car, accessible via the King Fahd Causeway.

The pitch was compelling. Respectfully, I remained politely on the sidelines.

SANDS OF GRATITUDE

The trip was winding down. By tomorrow afternoon, the journey home would begin, mercifully not via some emergency escape route with Bassel racing toward Damascus.

Before that, Omar had one final surprise, a farewell gift in the form of another adventure. We'd drive out to a more remote stretch of the desert, then ride camels a short distance to a traditional tent camp where we'd spend the night under the stars.

I was about to get a rare glimpse into the centuries-old Bedouin way of life.

Not a bad way to end a high-stakes business trip.

About an hour into the drive, the date palms disappeared behind us, replaced by the endless gold expanse of the Saudi desert.

There was a stillness, peaceful and profound, as we stepped out of the SUV and approached our next, slower-paced mode of transportation. Waiting for us was Abdullah, along with a small group of camels.

Standing easily over my head at 5'7", these animals were towering and regal, like desert royalty. Abdullah would be my handler. He shouted a command in Arabic, and my camel responded immediately, folding its legs beneath its body in one graceful, mechanical motion. It's remarkable how camels kneel, as if signaling, *permission granted*, though the grumbling sounds they make in the process suggest they're no pushover.

I swung one leg over the saddle and held on tight. The motion was jerky at first, but within seconds, I found myself high above the ground, ready to ride a camel through the Saudi desert. My companions mounted more gracefully.

Omar took the lead as we began our slow journey into the dunes. We weren't moving fast, but I preferred it that way. From that elevated vantage point, surrounded by silence and sand, the view was nothing short of surreal. It felt like we were on another planet. City life, with all its noise and modern conveniences, was nowhere in sight.

After a short ride, we arrived at our desert camp. A large tent stood waiting, woven fabric from top to bottom, open at the front. Inside, the furnishings were far more comfortable than anything you'd find at the neighborhood REI.

There was no running water. No electricity. Soon, though, there would be a fire.

The sun began to set. Having grown up along the beaches of Orange County, Southern California, and later calling the Central Coast of Santa Barbara home, I'd seen more than my fair share of breathtaking sunsets. Even so, this one would be etched in my memory forever.

The sky turned brilliant shades of pink and violet. The sand glowed in hues of gold and orange. For a brief moment, I thought about the upheaval not far from us, of impending war and deep uncertainty. In that moment, all I saw was boundless beauty. All I felt was endless gratitude. I made a wish for peace and offered a silent prayer.

Somehow, I hoped this experience, this gentle, humbling peace, was something I could carry with me, and share with the world.

With Omar and Bassel, going hungry was never a concern. Abdullah was now stationed at the fire, tending to a makeshift grill with pots suspended over the flames. Dinner that night would be lamb, rice, flatbread, and sweet tea, a desert feast under the open sky. By then, night had fallen fully across the dunes.

With no nearby cities to dull the view, the stars above us shone with a clarity I'd never experienced. They felt impossibly close. Flashes of light and the occasional shooting star danced across the sky like a celestial symphony. I'd always thought Joshua Tree or Yosemite offered the pinnacle of stargazing. This was in a league of its own.

The four of us sat cross-legged on rugs at the tent's opening, intimately sharing the meal Abdullah had prepared and swapping stories beneath that glowing canopy of stars. A few dim lanterns cast just enough light to accent the grace of the moment.

By now, the night air had cooled slightly, a sandy breeze offering some comfort, but it still felt very much like the desert. We ended the evening with Arabic coffee, which Bassel poured from an antique-looking *dallah* pot into our small cups, each about the size of an espresso shot. Arabic coffee is light and mild, blending perfectly with the desert air. Alongside it, we enjoyed local dates that Omar had brought along, rich and sweet, tasting almost like caramel. Then came a well-earned rest.

Waking up in the Arabian desert is something special. It's slightly windy and marks the coolest part of the day.

As beautiful as any sunset, the sunrise painted the desert in silver and blue, casting long shadows across the sand and against the tent. For me, it was the most peaceful moment, just before the rusty tones of the desert gave way to full daybreak and the return of the heat.

It was around this time that my companions calmly laid out their prayer rugs, each rug's orientation revealing the direction of Mecca from where we stood. Giving them privacy, I stepped away and took in my surroundings.

I was struck by how often the tradition and simplicity of desert life in this part of the world is viewed as something *less than*. Yet to me, it appeared, and felt, abundant.

After a simple breakfast of flatbread and cheese, along with another round of coffee, we said farewell to camp.

Retracing our steps led me back, and from there, I continued on to a layover near Dammam Airport. My flight home was
scheduled for the next morning, March 13, on the same route as
before, minus the stop in Kuwait.

It had been a journey that would stay with me for many
years to come. Countless memories. Meaningful takeaways. In retrospect, it may not have been the most prudent timing. Hard to say
if I would do it again. Thankfully, I made it home safely.

THE WISDOM TO KNOW THE DIFFERENCE

Not long after returning home, and while the trip's suc-
cesses were still echoing through the office, tragedy struck Saudi
Arabia. Whatever hope I had offered in the desert, it was no match
for what would unfold in Riyadh and the region. Just a week after
coming back, on March 20, 2003, the world watched as the U.S.-
led invasion of Iraq commenced, following Saddam Hussein's re-
fusal to relinquish power. *Operation Iraqi Freedom* had begun.

Less than two months later, on May 12, coordinated suicide
bombings targeted three residential compounds in Riyadh that were
known to house expatriates, the same kind of secure living quarters
that would have been used by our own employees had we gone
ahead with plans for a Saudi-based operation. The attacks claimed
35 civilian lives and injured over 160 others. In the wake of the
Riyadh bombings, we were forced to reassess the viability of
stationing staff in Saudi Arabia. The plant project was once again
shelved, this time, indefinitely.

That decision was only further validated as violence against
expats intensified throughout 2004. Additional attacks on compounds and worksites followed. In June of that year, an American

aerospace employee was abducted and brutally murdered in Riyadh. The message was clear, and our course of action, irreversible. The risks far outweighed the reward. The Saudi plant would never be built.

In the end, we made peace with what could not be changed, and walked away with the wisdom to know the difference.

The night in the desert would be the last time I saw Omar and Abdullah. Aside from a farewell at the airport, the same was true for Bassel.

Strangely enough, it wouldn't be the last I saw of Tariq.

HARVESTS TAKE TIME

A couple of years later, I was reminded of that wild trip to Saudi Arabia, this time in a very different setting.

At a petrochemical conference in Texas, I crossed paths with Tariq, the corporate executive who had once commended me for making the journey to Saudi during such a volatile time. He remembered our acquaintance.

We caught up during a reception he was hosting. He had relocated to Texas. Before long, that unexpected reunion turned into a working relationship, this time, not in Saudi Arabia, but right here at home.

Looking back, it's remarkable. I had traveled halfway around the world with a clear agenda to explore in-country manufacturing and sourcing opportunities. However, the greater value came years later, through a relationship formed on that trip, one that would evolve into a strategic supply alliance stateside, and continue for many years to come.

In business, we often focus on the immediate outcome, the deal closed, the problem solved, the metric moved. The real value sometimes comes later in ways we can't predict.

That trip to Saudi didn't lead to the result we originally envisioned, but it planted a seed. By showing up, building trust, and taking the time to genuinely connect, a relationship was formed that would bear fruit years later. It was a reminder that global business isn't just about transactions; it's about bridges. Bridges built on respect, curiosity, and a willingness to listen.

The best opportunities often grow from the groundwork we lay when no one's watching, with a vision flexible enough to adapt and a mindset open enough to let something unexpected take root.

4

THREE MOVES AHEAD:
A FIELD-TESTED FRAMEWORK FOR
CHANGE

In global business, the best-laid plans are rarely enough. Strategy only becomes real when it's tested, by shifting markets, supplier setbacks, geopolitical curveballs, and the thousands of everyday decisions that determine whether momentum builds or slips away. Introducing Protect. Pilot. Patch., a playbook refined on the ground, not in theory. A framework in motion, tested by fire and sharpened by failure. Built from instincts, not buzzwords. Whether the moment called for ninja-level agility, Gangnam-style diplomacy, karaoke ballads, or a spinning Lazy Susan, this journey traverses Italy, Korea, Malaysia, and Qatar to reveal how real change happens, not just with a plan on paper, but through fluid, adaptive motion. By the end, you'll see how supply chain bridges are built, why trust carries more weight than a cargo vessel, and how a simple field strategy, executed with precision, can turn uncertainty into advantage. The key takeaway? The biggest fish never bites first. Long-term solutions are assembled over time. And the path forward is almost never a straight line.

Up to this point, most of the stories have revolved around sourcing established products offshore or shifting suppliers to achieve better cost savings.

When specifications are already dialed in, global sourcing often becomes a race toward the lowest possible landed cost. The tariff battles of recent years, particularly those launched during both Trump Administrations, are a prime example. Products once reliably sourced from China became cost-prohibitive almost overnight due to layer upon layer of stackable tariffs. This pushed many businesses to explore new sourcing geographies.

What happens when you're not just looking to slap a logo on a ready-made design and ship it out the door? The so-called, "turnkey" scenario. What if you're developing something bespoke, built to spec, designed from scratch? That path can take a few sharp turns.

Sometimes, you already have a qualified supplier for the product category, but you're aiming to innovate. Other times, the product is so IP-sensitive that you split production across multiple factories, each handling a separate part, with final assembly done elsewhere. Or perhaps you manufacture in-house, but rely on a critical ingredient or component only produced by a small number of foreign suppliers. You might even come across a factory over-seas making a product your customers would love, with some tweaks to the design.

In any of these cases, you're not just sourcing, you're scouting, exploring, piecing together a vision.

Few places on Earth offer a better playground for that kind of creative pursuit than the Canton Fair. The Canton Fair, China's oldest and largest trade event, held in Guangzhou, has long been the go-to destination for product development inspiration. It has been referred to as the Silk Road of the 21st century, all under one colossal roof.

This isn't just another trade show. It's commerce on a different scale entirely. With over 1 million square feet of exhibition space, the fair draws hundreds of thousands of buyers from more than 200 countries, showcasing everything from robots to handbags, textiles to tech.

Wandering through the vast halls of this physical manifestation of Alibaba, surrounded by a bedazzle of flashing LED screens and a chorus of nearly every foreign language spoken on Earth, it's hard not to feel the creative sparks fly. If it doesn't get your product ideation flowing, you're simply not trying hard enough.

In a world increasingly reliant on Zoom calls and instant messages, the Canton Fair is a powerful reminder that the spirit of Alexandria and Athens still lives on in modern trade. Showing up still matters. Handshakes still seal deals. Just don't forget your best walking shoes, and stay hydrated.

Whatever path you take to reach your innovation objectives, the road map to a successful outcome requires reliable research findings, careful collaboration, reasonable transparency, and a strong foundation of trust.

The first stop was Milan, Italy. Before exploring potential sources for alternative fuels, I needed to meet with a key supplier of the current-spec fuel.

When mapping out this itinerary, the most efficient route unfolded as LA. to Milan, then to Kuala Lumpur, on to Doha, and finally back to LA., a full circumnavigation of the globe, with the final flight crossing over the Arctic. Beyond the novelty of the "round the world" milestone, the route had practical advantages, such as no backtracking. More importantly, flying west to east made adjusting to time zones more manageable. So yes, a traveler's badge of honor, but also a seasoned best practice.

My British Airways flight departed just after noon, with a layover in London. I'd land in Milan roughly 13 hours later, touching down around 10 a.m. local time the next day.

DE VINCI TO DEMAND PLANNING

After a smooth flight and short stopover, I checked into the Milan Marriott Hotel. With business not kicking off until 9 a.m. the following day, I had the afternoon to myself.

One personal mission on this trip was to finally see *Leonardo da Vinci's The Last Supper*. I had the foresight to book tickets in advance. Getting there required a short walk to the metro and a 20-minute subway ride.

The destination, Santa Maria delle Grazie, was an understated red-brick structure that didn't scream "world treasure," but once I arrived, I realized its humble architecture suited the subject matter. A functioning Dominican convent since 1497, the church was never meant to sparkle.

Inside, *The Last Supper* stretched across the wall of the former monks' dining hall, 15 feet high and 29 feet wide, painted in radiant detail directly onto the plaster. You don't just view the scene; you're absorbed into it. A sacred moment, shared across time. It was meaningful and meditative.

Still energized, I flagged a cab and made my way to the nearby Duomo.

A masterpiece of Gothic architecture, the Duomo stands as one of the most iconic cathedrals in the world. Inside, I wandered among towering marble columns and gazed up at storytelling stained-glass windows that filtered the afternoon light like divine kaleidoscope. Afterwards, I sat on the steps of the piazza out front and let the sights and sounds of the city settle in.

There were pigeons, many of them. A small mob of kids tossed crumbs, and more pigeons swooped in. Within minutes, the square teemed with flapping wings and laughing voices. It felt like a scene out of *The Godfather*. Had this been the marble steps of an opera house instead of a cathedral, I might've started scanning for a getaway route.

After a beautiful sunset over the piazza, I was ready to scout out a welcoming café for dinner. Guided only by my nose, I wandered just a short distance before coming across a lively pizzeria. It had a simple canopy overhead but otherwise offered open-air seating, perfect for enjoying the evening breeze and the endless entertainment of people-watching.

I ordered a Milanese-style pizza, listed as a personal size but easily stretching 12 inches across. A challenge I welcomed, having saved my appetite after the long journey in. My instincts leaned toward a New York-style approach of fold and go.

On second thought, I was in Milan after all. So, honoring the local custom I'd observed, I reached for a fork and knife and proceeded with the most refined approach to eating pizza I had ever attempted. Paired with a glass of Chianti, it was a literal slice of heaven.

After dinner, I had officially run out of gas. Experience has taught me that it's best to hit the pillow completely exhausted on the first night of an overseas trip for better odds of sleeping through the time difference and waking recharged.

Mission accomplished. I crashed on contact and woke feeling refreshed and ready to dive into the business of the visit. My first meeting was with a petrochemical company whose main operations are based in South Africa, but for this particular fuel product, Milan served as a key production site.

MANAGING MOLECULES

A company car had been arranged, and I was looking forward to finally meeting my primary contact in person. His name was Lorenzo. We'd worked together for years, but until now only across time zones and screens.

The ride was smooth, a black sedan weaving through Milan's café-lined streets and the usual river of scooters. Soon the city tapered off, replaced by blue road signs leading us toward the industrial outskirts.

We approached a sprawling complex. The hum of trucks and forklifts heard even before the gates. Distillation columns stood in the distance like silver sentinels. This was the place. At the front gate, I presented my passport and business card, and we were quickly waved through. We parked, and I made my way into the office building.

Lorenzo was waiting. I knew from past conversations that he was a passionate motorcyclist, and judging by the row of bikes parked out front, he wasn't alone in that obsession.

We exchanged warm pleasantries. Lorenzo was eager to show me around. I had the chance to meet several people from customer service and operations, familiar names, now with faces.

After the introductions, Lorenzo led us into a conference room where a couple of senior executives were waiting. I hadn't expected them, but appreciated that Lorenzo had taken the time to make the most of my visit.

From the outset, the tone was professional, welcoming, along with touches of refined hospitality Italy is known for.

We reviewed forecasts, and Lorenzo provided a strong overview of the state of the industry as it related to the highly specialized fuel product his company supplied to us.

While his presentation was well-delivered, it wasn't entirely rosy. Several major players had recently exited the market, leaving gaps in supply. That meant Lorenzo was now, hopefully, my new best friend.

The highlight of visits like these for me is always the up-close look at the operation itself. After passing safety screenings and suiting up in PPE, we were ready to tour the facility and see firsthand how the product was processed.

At this particular site, they weren't producing the chemical from raw feedstock, but rather refining and purifying imported material to meet specifications across a range of downstream consumer and industrial applications.

TRUST ON THE TABLE

The walkthrough was impressive, and it was clear Lorenzo was already thinking about lunch. That was fine by me. Italian food has always been a personal favorite, and I was more than ready. We headed out, not by motorbike as I half-expected, but back in the same black sedan I'd arrived in.

About 15 minutes later, we pulled up to something much more than a café. The restaurant stood on its own, a freestanding gem adorned with wrought-iron trellises laced in climbing ivy. Stone walls met greenery in a combination that felt both rustic and refined.

Lorenzo led the way, greeted immediately by name as we entered. "Your table is ready," said a man in a black bow tie and apron. We were shown to a table dressed in crisp linens, next to a large window overlooking a peaceful garden. Great choice, I thought.

This was clearly Lorenzo's show, and I was happy to follow his lead. Not just because he was the host, but because there's something to be said for watching a master at work.

"Sparkling wine before still," he explained with a grin. Then, with a casual flick of his hand, *"Ecco il vino!"* The wine appeared as if on cue.

Lorenzo raised his glass. "To loyal partners when it's easy, stronger allies when it's not—*Vecchi amici!*" The nod to old friends at the end was a nice touch, I thought.

He ordered for us, starting with an artichoke and parmesan salad, followed by something special, *Lavarello*, a freshwater white fish native to the lakes of Northern Italy. With another subtle exchange between Lorenzo and the sommelier, a chilled bottle of

Lugana appeared, a crisp, aromatic white wine he claimed was the perfect pairing for lake fish. He wasn't wrong.

We enjoyed the wine, and it was great catching up. The conversation drifted in and out of business, but given the global supply chain challenges at the time, Lorenzo made every effort to reassure me that we'd be taken care of. The key, he emphasized, would be accurate forecasting, critical for aligning with production schedules and materials planning.

What we were looking at, in industry terms, was *allocation*, meaning that our typical volumes would be covered, but anything beyond that was discretionary.

Knowing that others didn't even have it that good, I felt grateful for the relationship we'd built, one rooted in loyalty, trust, and transparency over many years. It's in moments like these when the investment pays dividends.

Then came the fish. It arrived on a rolling cart, escorted by a maître d'. The presentation was both impressive and slightly intimidating. The fish was whole, and quite large. It was deboned and seasoned with olive oil and herbs tableside for our viewing pleasure, then artfully plated.

We raised a more casual toast, *"cin cin,"* and enjoyed the full culinary experience. If this was how Italians did lunch, I thought, count me in.

Dessert followed, just as spectacular, and before we knew it, more than two hours had passed. Lorenzo explained that was customary in Italy. The pace is slower here, he added, something that felt to me more like a feature than a flaw.

OVER OCEANS TOWARD THE FUTURE

That concluded our time together. He dropped me back at my hotel, and I'd be flying out the next morning to Kuala Lumpur.

I felt good about the short visit to Milan.

In essence, it had been about shoring up supply, while also opening the door to explore longer-term opportunities, important given the circumstances. This stop was about "current state." The next two would move us toward "future state."

The focus of these next two visits would be to explore opportunities with a unique fuel product traditionally derived from crude oil but now being made from natural gas using an innovative process. Shifting to this fuel type promised a more secure long-term supply of a specialized fuel that was slowly vanishing from the market. It also offered cleaner environmental attributes thanks to the natural gas feedstock.

As a law school graduate, not an engineer, my strengths lay in logic and analysis rather than chemistry and physics. Still, the idea of learning, up close and in person, how Fischer-Tropsch synthesis transforms gas into liquid fuels felt oddly exciting. If nothing else, I figured that by the end of this trip I'd at least "know enough to be dangerous."

To make inroads with the chemical source in Malaysia, I'd partnered with a trading company I'd worked with before, one that had established relationships in the region.

The flight out of Milan was on Air India, connecting at about the half-way point, in Delhi. Then, I'd switch to Malaysia Airlines for the final flight to Kuala Lumpur.

I'd flown Malaysia Airlines before and had always enjoyed the onboard service, especially the chicken and beef satay served in business class. This trip took place in 2005, nine years before the airline would suffer two catastrophic disasters just months apart, one flight that vanished entirely, the subject of a Netflix documentary years later, and another shot down over Eastern Ukraine.

When it comes to my own anxiety about international flying, I'd call it a mixed bag. On one hand, the steady hum of the aircraft acts as white noise. It actually lulls me to sleep if I'm tired, making rest on long overseas flights usually no problem. On the other hand, crossing the Pacific Ocean demands certain respect.

As the largest and deepest body of water on Earth, the Pacific commands attention from 35,000 feet. Look out the window mid-flight and you're met with endless horizons in every direction. It's a view that makes the scale of the Earth feel undeniably real. Deep into a long-haul over that ocean, a sudden jolt or rattle from turbulence can be a stark reminder that you're not in the comfort or safety of your bedroom.

Flying over the Atlantic, while no puddle jump, somehow feels less ominous. Some consider the Pacific a "frontier" for its vast, unpredictable, and intimidating nature. Whereas, the Atlantic is more often thought of as a well trafficked "highway."

Both, are expansive enough to keep your senses on edge for the full 7 to 15 hours. Wine has the tendency to help.

In truth, after more than a hundred flights across these oceans, I've become consciously desensitized to the perils of air travel. What still shakes my nerves? Some of the car rides abroad, especially in the rural corners of Asia. Let's just say the roads in those regions weren't exactly built to Roman standards.

More often, they feel improvised rather than engineered, routes designed to test both your will... and your faith.

WARMTH IN HIGH PLACES

This time, the Malaysia Airline flight was perfect.

Upon landing, I swiftly moved through the airport and secured a cab. On the drive to the Banyan Tree Hotel, located in the heart of the city, the skyline unfolded with spectacular views of the iconic Petronas Twin Towers, stunning in their symmetry and rising with a sort of citadel-like prominence above the city.

Unfortunately, this trip didn't include a meeting with Petronas, Malaysia's state-owned oil giant the towers were named after. Maybe next time.

More than its architecture, what stands out quickly in Malaysia, especially in Kuala Lumpur, is its rich cultural diversity. The city hums with the daily interactions of Malays, Chinese, and Indians living and working side by side. Religious traditions blend too, with Islam, Buddhism, Hinduism, and others in a confluent mosaic.

From a culinary perspective, this diversity is a gift. Walk a single block and you can choose between Tandoori, Dim Sum, or Satay.

After checking in and resting a bit, I sprang to attention for my first mission, to meet up with my local host for the next couple of days. His name was Wei Bo, and we had plans for dinner at the Malaysia Petroleum Club, more than 40 floors up Tower 2 of the Petronas Towers.

It was a prestigious, members-only venue reserved for senior players in the oil and gas industry. Tonight, I would be Wei Bo's guest, and I'd do my best to be on my best behavior.

I decided to walk the 20 minutes from my hotel to the towers, using the time to explore a bit of the Golden Triangle, Kuala Lumpur's economic and social hotspot. The afternoon was warm, and the suit I'd chosen was no match for the humidity, it clung to me like shrink wrap.

Still, the walk had its charm. As I approached the base of the towers, I passed a grassy plaza full of local life, families on picnic blankets, kids running barefoot, couples sharing moments beneath the steel giants. It was a genuine, joyful contrast to the sleek corporate world just floors above.

Inside, I wandered through the multi-level shopping center mostly to cool off in the air-conditioning and dry out before dinner.

After a short walk and a quick orientation, I reached the security checkpoint for the Petroleum Club. Access required clearance and a confirmed guest list. Thankfully, I was on it.

The elevator ride was fast. When the doors opened, I stepped into a polished reception area where a hostess greeted me by name, a small but striking detail that reminded me this would be an evening of unspoken formality.

Just then, Wei Bo rounded the corner with a grin, a hand extended, and the kind of warm confidence that only comes from knowing exactly where you stand. He was clearly well known here.

We exchanged greetings, and I thanked him for the special invitation. With a quick nod, he let me know that a couple of his friends would be joining us. "Hope you don't mind," he said. "Of course not," I replied.

As we stepped into the main dining area, the club revealed itself in stages, floor-to-ceiling windows offering panoramic views of the KL skyline, tables arranged with deliberate spacing, and bright orchids adding just the right touch of life and color.

A soft piano melody drifted in the background, blending with the steady hum of conversation and the delicate clink of glass on glass. I couldn't help but wonder how many oil deals had been sealed here over glasses of aged Scotch and silent nods.

Wei Bo introduced me to Jian Hao, and then to a sharply dressed man with an easy smile, introduced simply as Richard. I would soon learn that Richard, locally branded as an Asian Richard Gere, was the one who'd bring the energy to the table. A few hours later, I'd be convinced Richard came across more like an Asian *J.R. Ewing*.

Champagne was already waiting. We toasted my arrival. I felt genuinely honored, and excited for the business planned over the next couple of days. We were seated in a corner next to the window, what felt to me as the best spot in the house.

As the sun slipped behind the hills, the skyline glowed, and the room took on a warm radiance that slowly faded into candle-light. A server arrived with a bottle of whiskey from what appeared to be Richard's private reserve, and his clear intent was to generously share.

As our candle flickered gently in its holder, Richard raised his glass and gave a toast that fit the moment and setting perfectly, "Here's to full glasses and rising fortunes… may we drill deep and drink well." We dined, and dug deep, into conversation and into Richard's bottle.

Afterward, Wei Bo kindly offered me a ride back to my hotel. We said goodnight with a handshake and a promise to reconnect in the morning. Grateful for the company and the experience, I was more than ready to call it a night.

It was already forming into a trip to remember.

THE CATALYST EFFECT

The next morning, Wei Bo was waiting in the lobby, ready for the journey ahead. First, we'd make our way back to Kuala Lumpur International Airport, followed by a two-hour flight across the South China Sea to the town of Bintulu, in Sarawak.

Once we landed, the change in scenery was immediate, lush tropical rainforest, coastal mangroves, and humid air that felt heavier, wilder than what we'd left behind in KL. From there, it was another hour by car, a drive that would take us deep into Sarawak, the heart of Malaysia's natural gas industry. We'd be staying overnight on this side of the country.

When we finally arrived, the view was something to behold. Rows of oil palm trees lined the hills, stretching across the landscape like a grid imposed on nature. Just beyond, untamed jungle rose thick and defiant.

Peeking through, tucked between the palms and the forest, stood the unmistakable imprint of industry, towering steel columns, flare stacks, and a maze of pipes, all rising like a metallic city pulled from the forest floor.

It was industry and jungle in a kind of tense harmony, a meeting point between precision and wilderness. It was precisely what I had traveled all this way to see first-hand.

Wei Bo had proven himself the man about campus on this trip. Just like the club, his presence had drawn together an impressive group of executives, who met us in front of the conference room reserved for our meeting.

For the first fifteen minutes or so, Wei Bo held court, speaking mostly in Mandarin, occasionally dropping an English word for flair. The banter was unmistakable.

Clearly familiar with these executives both in and out of the office, he launched into an exaggerated golf swing demonstration. He might've been imitating himself, or someone else entirely, but I couldn't quite follow the full exchange. Still, with body language and keywords in English like "slice" and "power" thrown in, I was able to pace just close enough to catch the gist.

Then it became crystal clear when Wei Bo turned to me and grinned. "This guy… he brings driver, but no license." Laughter erupted. We were off to a great start, thanks to Wei Bo softening the tone and setting the stage.

It reminded me of the importance of choosing the right partner when navigating a tough sourcing landscape, especially one riddled with hidden barriers, cultural nuance, and uncertain footing.

Someone wise told me once, that markets are like the lotus. They don't bloom for just anyone. They open for those who know when not to reach, those who understand its nature and approach just right. Wei Bo was clearly our lotus whisperer in this prospective deal. Too early to tell where it would lead, but the tone was right. And that mattered.

Years later, during my own experience in Japan, I had started off much the same as now, just a guest at the table during an early visit. After some rounds on the golf course together over years following, with more than a few wayward shots and shared laughs about stubborn sand traps, our formal connections softened into genuine friendships. By the time we had reunions, the banter flowed effortlessly. The laughter was familiar, the friendly interaction the same.

Relationships form, and if you're lucky, they stick. Sometimes, you even become the local whisperer yourself.

If it's up to me in these kinds of situations, I'll stand behind someone like Wei Bo every time. Pay the finder's fee, the broker fee, whatever it takes to get a well-footed start, within legal and ethical boundaries of course. Because someone truly qualified isn't just a charmer. They usually bring in-country distribution and logistics muscle too, which can make the difference when it comes to actual execution. They can also intervene when problems arise.

Every situation stands on its own, with its nuance, novelty, and surprises, but in sourcing, like in golf, when you link up with the right partner, that's hitting the sweet spot.

As we settled around the table, the conversation flowed naturally. There was no formal slide deck, this visit was meant to be more informal.

The discussion focused mostly on how the fuel was produced, and what aspects of the process led to significantly better combustion emissions compared to its crude oil-based counterpart. From a basic chemistry standpoint, the end products were classified the same, but the performance differences were substantial.

It was an engaging meeting, and now, we'd begin the plant tour, which I was most looking forward to.

Wei Bo and I watched a safety video, suited up in coveralls, hard hats, earplugs, and safety glasses, and made our way outside. A member of the production team was waiting to guide us along a designated pathway.

We started at the feedstock intake area, where natural gas is piped in from offshore fields. There were brief stops and slow walks past the early stages of the process, but soon we reached the moment I'd been waiting for, the Fischer-Tropsch stage, where the real magic happens.

Inside tall reactors, cleaned synthesis gas flows over a solid catalyst, triggering chemical reactions that produce long-chain liquid hydrocarbons.

As Wei Bo explained it in lay terms, the reactor worked like a bakery oven, the catalyst was the baking tray, the syngas the batter. Add heat, and out comes the bread, or in this case, a paraffin-like substance. After further refining, it becomes the finished, usable product.

It was a fascinating tour.

SET CHAIRS, SPINNING TABLE

As we wrapped up, it was about lunchtime, and Tan Kai, who had been our leading point of contact throughout, assumed the role of host and invited us to join him in a waiting car.

Today's meal would be Chinese, and a private room was already prepared at a nearby restaurant.

As we entered the room, A TV played the local news in the background. There were about six of us in total. I've always found the formalities of Chinese business meals fascinating. As we entered, Tan Kai took the seat closest to the wall, facing the door, considered the host's position, with the best view of the room. He motioned for me to sit on his right, the traditional spot reserved for the guest of honor. Wei Bo was invited to sit on his left. The others took their seats in what appeared to be a deliberately arranged order.

This seating hierarchy has roots in Confucian principles of respect and social harmony, and meals like this reflect that tradition. Food was served family-style, with dishes placed on a glass Lazy Susan in the center of the table.

Tan Kai occasionally spun it toward me to highlight a dish worth trying. There was beef with black pepper, local fish, roasted chicken, and a variety of vegetable sides. Dishes didn't all arrive at once. They were brought out gradually and placed on the rotating tray as they were ready.

Before long, the table was filled with a generous offering, much of which would be packed up afterward for others back at the office. Conversation during meals like this typically stay away from business, focusing more on getting to know one another personally.

Much of today's discussion centered around Hurricane Katrina, which had struck the Gulf Coast just weeks earlier. The devastation to the oil and gas industry had been severe, with offshore platforms, pipelines, drilling rigs, and refineries all suffering heavy damage.

Tan Kai mentioned knowing people at affected operations in coastal Louisiana, though fortunately, he reported, there were no injuries. Despite the somber topic of Katrina, there was a shared appreciation for resilience, both in people and in industries forced to recover quickly.

As the meal progressed, the conversation drifted to family, hometowns, and a few lighthearted stories from past travels.

Just as the assortment of tropical fruit and sweet lotus seed pastries arrived, the clear signal that the meal was winding down, Tan Kai lifted the mood.

He'd become a huge fan of *The Apprentice*. Grinning, he mimicked Donald Trump's trademark line, pointing across the table with mock authority, "You're fired!" The impression was spot-on. We all laughed, and he explained how addictive the show had become for him. "Very strong leader. Knows what he wants," he said, nodding with genuine admiration.

With a final toast of jasmine tea, we wrapped up the meal. Shortly after, we were on our way back to the office.

BRIDGES AND BEGINNINGS

We had accomplished the objectives of this introductory visit, and after a quick recap back at the office, Wei Bo and I offered our thanks for the warm hospitality and the generous amount of time spent with us.

The conversation wouldn't end here; we agreed to keep exploring possibilities as our plans took clearer shape.

Some upcoming production modifications at the factory looked promising and could bring things closer in line with the fuel spec we had in mind.

That evening, we stayed at the Promenade Hotel in Bintulu, just a few miles from the airport. Wei Bo was heading to Singapore the next morning, and I was flying back to KL. We said our good-byes that night. I thanked him for everything and complimented the work he'd done. I told him I'd follow up after the trip with ideas on next steps.

It's customary in Asia to exchange a small gift, nothing extravagant, just a token of appreciation. Over the weeks leading up to the trip, Wei Bo and I had gotten to know each other fairly well through long Skype calls.

As it turned out, we both had something to give the other, for our kids. I gave him a small Disney toy for his son. He, in turn, presented me with a beautifully carved wooden dragon for my daughter. She was born in the year of the Dragon.

FUEL FOR THOUGHT

Next stop, Doha, Qatar.

A seven-and-a-half-hour flight from KL, landing at what was then the old Doha Airport, long before the sleek, architectural marvel that is Hamad International came online.

Stepping outside, just beyond the doorway, you're met by a heatwave so steady and unrelenting, it instantly affirms why the desert never embraced the necktie.

A line of white Land Cruisers awaited. I quickly climbed into one and began taking in the sights. Doha's skyline was very different from my last time in the region, having previously visited Dubai and Abu Dhabi.

Here, the skyline stretched across a canvas of sand, glass towers rising high into the sky, curiously spaced apart. Doha still had room to grow, and the world seemed eager to help.

The first two days of this visit were devoted to a petroleum conference. If you can fold an industry event into a sourcing trip, I've always found it worth the effort. The right ones deliver insight and strategy you won't find in trade magazines. If a new process or product was generating real buzz, especially one tied directly to where I was standing, then yes, it was worth an extra day or two to listen, observe, and learn what hides behind the curtain of official press releases.

This particular conference was held at the Ritz-Carlton, which exceeded my travel budget by several levels. I stayed at the Sheraton instead, just a 10-minute cab ride away.

The speaker lineup was impressive, including high-ranking Qatari government officials from the Ministry of Economy and Commerce, the Ministry of Energy and Industry, and even representatives from the Supreme Council for Economic Affairs and Investment, chaired by the Crown Prince.

Top execs from the biggest global oil and gas firms were also present, many of them showcasing mega-scale projects that rivaled the size of New York's Central Park.

Attending? A who's-who of the global petroleum world. This was the kind of venue where you could practically hear echoes of Rockefeller, Getty, and Pickens, laying out the next energy frontier, right here in the Qatari desert.

It was one of the most compelling conferences I've ever attended. I walked away with clarity, insight, and a firm belief that this was the right time, and the right place, to be exploring alternative fuel sources.

The investment dollars were flowing. The innovation was real. Too many geopolitical and commercial forces were in play for Qatar not to become the epicenter of natural gas innovation well into the foreseeable future, especially given demand from Japan, South Korea, India and Europe.

The U.S. would eventually come into play, but at that time, it wasn't the primary driver.

FUTURE IN THE MAKING

With my head spinning from two full days of briefings, panels, and hallway conversations, the final meeting of the trip was with one of the major project stakeholders, an executive representing what would soon become one of the world's largest gas-to-liquids plants.

The facility hadn't been built yet, but when completed, it would produce over 750,000 metric tons annually of high-performance synthetic fuels derived from natural gas.

At the time, only South Africa's coal-based processes surpassed those numbers.

This was long before ESG initiatives took hold in corporate America or greenhouse gas reporting and standard practices emerged. Intently now, the seeds were being planted, and the signs were clear, change was coming.

Our conversation was candid. We discussed product grade ranges, carbon chain targets, and technical specs. The fuel we were interested in wouldn't be among the first batches, higher-demand markets would be served first, but it was encouraging to hear that our spec was already in the roadmap.

We stayed in touch in the years that followed, and eventually, we did qualify the fuel. That initial conversation was the foundation. It was time well spent.

ECHOES OF TRADE

With business handled, I had some free time. This was my first visit to Qatar, and I wanted to get a better feel for the country.

I arranged a trip to Al Zubarah Fort, a drive of about an hour and a half through the desert. The Land Cruiser arrived and I jumped in.

Soon, the skyline disappeared in the rearview. We passed herds of goats led by sun-worn shepherds, gas stations that looked like mirages, and not much else. Eventually, the outline of the fort appeared on the horizon, slowly revealing itself, square layout, towers on each corner, standing resolute against the sand and wind.

Constructed in the 1930s from coral limestone, the fort itself had never seen combat, though the land it stood on had history.

Al Zubarah had once been one of the Gulf's most significant trading hubs. Surrounded now by dry desert, its main attraction back then was pearls, harvested from the nearby Persian Gulf. The shallow reefs of northwest Qatar had been bountiful grounds for pearl diving, and Zubarah was the anchor point.

The visit was memorable, made even more so by the contrast between ancient commerce and the new energy frontier I'd been immersed in for days.

I returned to the Sheraton at dusk, tired but content. I'd fly out the next morning.

This was an all-together different kind of trip, part present, part future. The objectives were layered, shore up existing supply, and scout promising alternatives. Both were essential. With storm clouds gathering around current sources, the excitement of future opportunities is tempting, but risk must be managed.

Over time, I'd formalize this philosophy into what I call the 3P Supply Framework: Protect. Pilot. Patch.

Protect the present. Pilot the future. Patch the gaps. Simple, maybe. Yet it works.

PROTECT. PILOT. PATCH.

PROTECT — Protect the present. — **MILAN**

PILOT — Pilot the future. — **KUALA LUMPUR & DOHA**

PATCH — Patch the gaps. — **SEOUL**

GANGNAM STYLE

The trip to Milan was intended to *protect*, the trips to Kuala Lumpur and Doha, *pilot* and one I had planned in a month to Seoul, would be strategically focused on *patch*.

Although Milan helped safeguard against a near-term supply crunch, it didn't account for future demand growth. As a single solution, it still left us a bit exposed.

That's what brought me to South Korea about a month later, where another source for the specialty fuel, smaller in scale, but promising, was worth a closer look. The Korean option wouldn't match current or future volumes from our primary suppliers, but as a supplemental source, it could bridge the gap between our historical allocations and what the forecasts were starting to show.

The direct flight from LAX to Seoul was just under 13 hours and, thankfully, uneventful. I'd be meeting a long-time contact on this visit, not a first-time introduction like Wei Bo in Malaysia.

His name was Park, but among American friends he simply went by Jason. Educated in the U.S., fluent in both English and business in Korea, Jason was one of those rare intermediaries who made everything smoother.

He also happened to be an exceptional host, and had strong ties to the petroleum producer we planned to visit.

It had been a while since we'd seen each other, either in Korea or stateside. We blocked off the evening before our visit to catch up over dinner. Among my favorite culinary experiences anywhere is Korean BBQ, and Jason knew just the place.

About a 20-minute drive from where I was staying, Samwon Garden offered the perfect blend of elegance, authenticity, and open flame. I had checked in earlier to the JW Marriott in Gangnam, an excellent choice in Seoul's trendiest district.

Whenever I think of Gangnam, I can't help but recall the cultural phenomenon that would come years later, "Gangnam Style," and the electric-walking *Psy* toy I bought for my son on a later trip. Dressed in a black tuxedo and perpetually mid-dance, the toy would hop and shuffle endlessly to that now-infamous tune.

For one whole summer, *Psy* was practically family, until, tragically, he walked himself right into our swimming pool. Turns out, he didn't have all the right moves. Back in 2005, Gangnam was still posh and stylish…just not world-famous yet.

Jason was already waiting in the lobby. We were off. The drive to the restaurant passed through the neon-lit streets of Seoul before giving way to a more refined setting. We passed through a stone gate, lined by manicured hedges, koi ponds, and glowing paper lanterns. The restaurant's exterior, complete with a traditional hanok roof, looked more like a royal residence than a place to get grilled meat in the city.

Once inside, the mood was warm and serene, timeless Korea with modern refinement. Jason had reserved a private room, thoughtful as always.

He ordered for us, and I knew exactly what to expect, *Galbi* and *Samgyeopsal*. Jason added a surprise treat, *Hanwoo* beef, Korea's prized native cattle, with marbling that rivals Wagyu. The table soon filled with banchan, the small plates that begin every Korean meal. Cucumber slices, several varieties of kimchi, and my personal favorite, *Gamja Jorim*, sweet and tender braised potatoes.

As the grill warmed, Jason ordered soju, and not just any bottle, a premium, corked version. He poured the first glass, and I instinctively followed protocol, refilling his in return.

Then came the first toast. Jason raised his glass and smiled. "To old friends reunited, to good health, better luck, and more layovers than hangovers." *Geonbae!*

We were officially off… on what would lead to our first hangover, I imagined.

The food started arriving, and the rest of the evening followed a familiar pattern of grilling, pouring and storytelling. Soju tends to steer the conversation from polite to animated rather quickly, and this night was no exception. We laughed, caught up on life, and traded business war stories.

We wrapped the meal with *Kimchi Jjigae*, a bubbling pot of kimchi stew with tofu and vegetables, served alongside a bowl of rice. I always like to mix my rice straight into the soup, letting the textures combine.

Kimchi, to Koreans, is far more than food. It's cultural pride, a daily ritual, and, some would say, a form of medicine. In fact, during the 2003 SARS epidemic, some in Korea casually credited the country's low infection rate to kimchi's immune-boosting powers. Myth or not, it was just one more reason to enjoy every last bite.

Jason arranged a car to take me back. He lived nearby. We'd meet again in the morning and head south together to Ulsan, home to the plant that, if all went well, might just become the final piece of our 3P supply puzzle.

THE ROAD TO REFINEMENT

The next morning came quickly, par for the course with overseas travel. Gratefully hangover-free, I sent a silent thanks to Jason for ordering the premium soju the night before.

Jason was already waiting in the car outside the hotel. I hopped in, and we pulled away from Gangnam, heading toward Ulsan, a steady four-hour drive. These long road trips often double as the perfect time to catch a power nap, and I made good use of the opportunity.

We cruised out of Seoul and left the city behind. The neon and bustle gave way to serene countryside, rolling green hills, pockets of rice paddies, and cherry trees dotting the horizon. I drifted in and out of sleep, answered a few emails, and chatted with Jason between stretches of silence.

Eventually, the countryside gave way to something else entirely, the unmistakable reemergence of commerce. This was no suburban sprawl. It was South Korea's industrial engine coming into view.

Ulsan, a deep-water port city and a global trade corridor, pulses with the energy of a world-class oil and gas hub. Tankers lined the coast. Trucks rumbled past in all directions. Railcars, distillation towers, and storage tanks filled the skyline.

Every inch of the horizon seemed busy doing something energetic. We passed through the security gate of one of the most impressive refineries in the cluster.

As we stepped out of the car, a mixture of sea mist and refinery haze filled the air, an unmistakable scent of hydrocarbons and salt that let you know business was about to begin.

NINJA MOVES

Jason had done a stellar job laying the groundwork for this visit. As we walked into the office lobby, a digital welcome sign displayed my name, a nice personal touch that set the tone before we even reached the reception desk. The lobby itself looked more like a five-star airport lounge, with leather couches and armchairs that might've been Italian.

As cozy as it appeared, I had a rule about lobbies. One of my early mentors drilled it into me by saying, "The person you're meeting isn't behind that door lounging in a leather chair reading a magazine, so you shouldn't be either."

His advice was clear, stand tall, look sharp, and be ready the moment they come out. That lesson stuck. So, while the reception-ist politely invited me to sit, I opted instead to study the walls. There was no shortage of achievements on display, framed awards, ISO certifications, and a large, glass-encased scale model of the refinery that pulled me in for a closer look.

It didn't take long before Min-Jae Kim arrived. Late fifties, sharp suit, confident walk, he carried the poise of someone who'd seen Korea's oil and gas sector through multiple eras of transfor-mation. He greeted Jason first, then turned to me and said in polished English, "Welcome, Mr. Jarrod."

"Please, call me Jarrod," I replied. "It's a pleasure to be here. Thank you for making the time." "I am Min-Jae," he said with a grin. "Like "ninja," he added, mimicking a playful karate chop. It was a small moment, but a welcome one. Ice officially broken.

As expected in Asia, the formalities continued with a two-handed business card exchange, thumbs pressed at the corners, as if presenting a gift.

There's a ritual to it, and I always respected that. This wasn't Vegas, you don't just snap a card out of someone's hand and toss one back like a blackjack dealer.

I took his card carefully, read it, noted his title, and offered a small nod of respect. I returned the gesture with a card of my own, also offered with two hands. One side in English, the reverse in Korean. It's a small investment, printing local-language cards, but one that always pays off.

He flipped it to the Korean side, smiled, and gave me the same nod I'd just given him.

As the saying goes, "you never get a second chance to make a first impression."

TOUR GUIDE STATUS

With greetings complete, we followed Min-Jae into a conference room where a presentation was already queued up. Five others were seated at the table, and after brief introductions, Min-Jae launched into the company history.

The operation had been part of Korea's national energy strategy, beginning as a full-scale crude refinery, expanding into petrochemicals and lubricants, and now ranked among the world's most integrated and efficient facilities.

Then came the tour. By this point, refinery number four in just a few weeks, I was inching beyond "just dangerous enough to know something." I could probably deliver parts of the tour myself.

That was by design. I wanted to be immersed, to know the people, the processes, the blind spots, so that my instincts were grounded in something more than theory.

What stood out here was the sheer level of automation. Machines moved cargo like clockwork. Sensors and lights blinked at every turn. Nothing was left unmeasured, and no process too small to monitor.

This facility felt like a control room with a refinery attached.

FISHING NOT CATCHING

As we returned to the conference room, Min-Jae didn't waste time tiptoeing around the reality of the situation. A seasoned pro, he wasn't about to make empty promises or try to sell what he didn't have.

That's rare in global sourcing, where even in the most constrained markets, suppliers tend to nod along with a confident, "No problem, we can do it," even when it's clear they can't. Min-Jae was different. He laid it out plainly, his hands were tied for now. The product spec we needed was currently oversold.

Not without moves, a Ninja after all, he said there *could* be an opportunity a few months down the road, once a large project wrapped up. My instincts, by now sharpened from weeks of refinery visits and supplier meetings, told me this wasn't just polite deflection. There was a real chance here.

Without a healthy amount of patience, fortitude, and an open mind, in this line of work, you'll hit a wall before you hit your stride. Especially when you're chasing innovation.

It's more fishing than catching, and that's okay. The biggest fish never bites first. We agreed to stay in touch. As luck, or creative scheduling, would have it, we both had upcoming travel to Shanghai. I may have fudged my original plans a bit, mine was actually the following week, but I flexed my schedule to align with his.

It's always better to keep these relationship-building conversations going face to face, especially while the momentum is fresh. We said our goodbyes and parted on great terms.

Jason and I had one more night in Ulsan before we'd say our farewells.

POWER BALLADS

After checking into our hotel, we regrouped and hopped back in the car, looking to unwind someplace casual, recap the business, and mix in a little fun.

Jason suggested a Hof near the harbor he knew well; a Korean take on a German beer hall.

Right away, it felt more local than the internationally styled bars you'd find back in Itaewon, Seoul's cultural hot spot similar to Hong Kong's Lan Kwai Fong. The Hof had its own charm, a long wooden bar, walls decorated in tribute to Korea's national soccer team, and an impressive selection of both domestic and international beers on tap.

K-pop and '90s American R&B played in rotation, a mashup that shouldn't have worked but did. We split a pitcher of Cass beer and a plate of crispy fried chicken with fries.

Jason, it turned out, had been in a rock band growing up, and naturally had a favorite karaoke spot 'nearby' in every town. Ulsan was no exception.

For someone with my singing abilities, at best described as off-key, these places were generally off-limits. My wife occasionally sang in a band growing up, and two of our kids are accomplished musical theater performers. It's not unusual for our living room to turn into a full-blown opera house at any given moment.

Me? I'm the guy lip-syncing show tunes on family road trips. Karaoke isn't exactly where I shine. Hence, I usually made every effort to avoid these places.

However, Jason was persuasive, and it was just a short walk away. He led us to the counter, gave the nod, "Two people, private room." The hostess handed him a call button for drink service, and we were escorted to our setup, a U-shaped leather couch, microphones, massive TV, a songbook the size of an old-school phone directory, and a disco ball overhead.

I couldn't help but think of Bill Murray in *Lost in Translation*, which I had watched on the plane.

Jason opened strong with *Misty Mountain Hop* and absolutely crushed it. I could've sworn Robert Plant was in the room.

That night, convinced I was among friends, even if just one, and after a few generous pours of Cass, *Yellow Submarine* and *My Way* started sounding manageable.

Meanwhile, Jason was fronting *Metallica* and *Iron Maiden* like the camera was rolling. He closed with *Sweet Child o' Mine*, and with that, our audition for VH1's Behind the Music was winding down.

We wrapped up a night to remember and headed back to the hotel.

That would be the last time I'd see Jason for a few years, until our paths crossed again in LA.

Even then, it was like no time had passed. A quick greeting of, *"Welcome to the Jungle"* ... and we were off to the next adventure.

ASSEMBLED OVER TIME

A few months later, just as we'd planned, I met up with Min-Jae for coffee at the Grand Hyatt in Shanghai. The project he'd hinted at was beginning to wind down.

A month later, our first shipment of on-spec fuel was on its way. Paired with our guaranteed supply, we were finally in position, not just to cover our needs, but to weather the unknown until future innovations materialized, as projected.

The visit to Korea marked the final bend in what I'd come to see as an arc, not just of travel, but of innovation.

Milan had been about protecting what we had. Malaysia and Doha offered a glimpse into what was coming. And Ulsan? Ulsan was the bridge, the piece that connected present to future.

In global sourcing, progress doesn't always come in the form of a breakthrough, almost never a straight line. Sometimes, it's an arc you build piece by piece.

5

FOOTNOTES FROM THE FIELD: LESSONS LEARNED, NOT TAUGHT

Some lessons don't come from leadership seminars or the latest management must-read. Welcome to the field, where the ground game begins, and the real test of leadership starts, navigating teams, terrain, and truths that don't come with a manual. These insights were earned by digging deeper, asking sharper questions, and staying long enough to see what others missed. What's revealed? How ecosystems behave in business, how history subtly repeats itself, and how influence is built, not through titles, but through presence. These aren't classroom lessons. They're the kind written in the margins of experience, and walked out, one footnote at a time. Whether it's a clever seatbelt workaround, borrowed wisdom from the Qing Dynasty, gently steering your way through fish of all sizes, or pausing just long enough to appreciate the legacy behind what's on tap in front of you, this is a glimpse into the mindset of the farmer and the fisherman… not the fry cook.

I was tasked with leading a strategic initiative to offshore a range of packaging components and turnkey items spanning multiple categories and market channels, including both industrial and consumer products.

The scale was massive, hundreds of SKUs that would require coordinating with no fewer than a dozen suppliers.

GROUND GAME BEGINS

After several sourcing trips through China and across Asia, the landscape had started to take shape.

We had a good sense of which regions to target for which product categories. The clarity on geography addressed part of the complexity. It was clear that to execute this initiative properly, we'd need significant on-the-ground support.

Managing that scale remotely from the U.S., with a fifteen-hour time difference, meant winding down on the West Coast just as China's workday was beginning. Coordination would rely on early-morning or late-night Skype calls, depending on which side of the Pacific you were on, which wasn't practical.

Intent on bridging the gaps led me to open an export office in Shanghai. To start, it would be a lean operation, just a couple of team members working remotely, with access to a shared conference room for supplier meetings. We'd also have a quality inspector who would oversee new supplier qualification and inspect shipments throughout the supplier network.

I'd travel out monthly to assess prospective suppliers, manage supplier onboarding, cover any trouble that was surfacing. I had a good contact in China's oil and gas sector from previous work together on paraffin supply. He was well connected, someone who knew the right circles, even if he wasn't suited to run day-to-day operations.

He introduced me to someone who was very capable and enthusiastic. That someone was Steven.

The office was located in Pudong, near Shanghai's international airport, inside a Free Trade Zone (FTZ). At the time, we didn't fully take advantage of its trade benefits, but it gave us options down the road to streamline Customs clearance, defer, and in some cases avoid, duties for some assembly work.

I landed on a Sunday night via Cathay Pacific. I was there to spend a few weeks on the ground with Steven.

Our agenda was packed, a Herculean itinerary across China, including Ningbo, Zhuhai, Wuxi, Qingdao, Beijing, Tianjin, and Dalian. In directional terms, we were covering China's coastline end-to-end, from the Pearl River Delta in the south to the Yellow Sea in the north.

This trip, and many more like it in the years that followed, laid the foundation of what would become my global playbook. Over time, I'd go on to visit nearly every major commercial city in China, as well as fifteen other countries across Southern, Southeast, and East Asia.

In those days, I usually stayed at Shanghai's Grand Hyatt inside the Jin Mao Tower. At the time, it was the tallest hotel in the world, over 1,300 feet high. The Cloud 9 Lounge on the 87th floor offered a panoramic view that revealed the city in its entirety when the skies cooperated.

Shanghai in the early-to-mid 2000s was growing at full tilt, a city under constant construction.

THE ECO SYSTEM EFFECT

Our first stop was Ningbo.

Back then, without the Hangzhou Bay Bridge, the drive took about five hours. Today, it's half that.

Ningbo is the national hub for flammable gas products, lighters, camping fuel, and similar goods, not by chance, but by design. Certain areas were specially zoned for chemical and hazardous goods production. Once the first cluster of gas-product factories reached critical mass, the ecosystem formed around it, with metal canister suppliers, valve manufacturers, injection molding shops, and leak-testing system vendors, all within driving distance of one another. Add to that Ningbo's position as one of the busiest ports in the world, with economies of scale for dangerous goods cargo, and you had a textbook example of China's regional supply chain ecosystems.

These hubs give buyers the advantage of concentrated sourcing of multiple factories in close proximity, all producing variations of the same product.

OXFORDS AND JORDANS

Steven and I spent a couple days visiting lighter factories. We gathered samples, evaluated capabilities, and sent everything back for marketing to review.

He was great to work with, late 20s, sharp, confident, and very capable. He held a mechanical engineering degree from one of the prestigious universities in China. Yet, Steven was far from the stereotype of a stiff, reserved engineer. He was extremely tall, at least 6'5", and had played in competitive basketball leagues during his time in school.

He had presence, calm focus, and a sense of humor that made long days on the road a lot more enjoyable.

Steven's only real vice was his obsession with sneakers, especially high tops. He was a connoisseur of Air Jordans.

I remember on one factory visit in particular, I was in my usual oxfords, standing next to Steven in his *Cool Grey Jordans*, with some yellow bling in the stitching.

When we walked in, heads turned. The two of us made quite the pair, me at 5'7" and him towering overhead.

We looked like Arnold Schwarzenegger and Danny DeVito in *Twins*.

This time, we were staying at the new Shangri-La hotel, overlooking an intersection between three rivers. That evening, we stopped into the Lobby Lounge, where a jazz duo played softly in the background.

Our appraisal of the day was on point. We'd left no stone unturned when it came to lighters and gas canisters. Tomorrow, the road trip would continue. Our next stop was Wuxi, about a six-hour drive north, crossing the Yangtze River Delta.

Wuxi is home to eastern China's largest freshwater lake. When in season, the mitten crab from Lake Tai is one of China's most sought-after delicacies, so prized, in fact, that counterfeit crabs have become a real problem. It was early October, right in the heart of crab season. We'd be in for a treat.

We had a different car and driver lined up for this leg of the trip. It was an early start. Steven and I met in the lobby at 6 a.m., aiming to reach one of the factories on our list shortly after lunch.

A dark blue Buick minivan pulled up out front. The driver was far more energetic than either of us. He greeted us with a broad smile, helped load our bags, and we were off, coffees in hand for the road.

DRILLING INTO LOOPHOLES

I'm not one to need reminding to buckle up, especially in China. I always do at home, and abroad it feels doubly important. So, I clicked in without thinking.

However, a couple minutes down the road, I heard that familiar "ding, ding, ding," the universally recognizable seatbelt warning. I glanced behind me. Steven was already asleep, head tilted back, somehow brushing the roof of the van. He was buckled up.

That's when the driver and I locked eyes. We realized, at the exact same moment, it was *him* setting off the alarm. I gave a polite nod toward the buckle, just a small gesture.

What happened next, has stayed with me years later. Apparently, he'd forgotten his trick. Without saying a word, he reached into the door compartment and pulled out a contraption, basically the chrome-plated tongue of a seatbelt, attached to about an inch of nylon webbing. Just enough to grip.

He inserted it into the buckle.

"Ding, ding, ding" and silence.

He leaned back, beaming with pride, as if he'd just solved a puzzle. I couldn't help but wonder why he didn't just buckle up to be safe? Instead, he'd taken time and effort to engineer a workaround. I had six hours to reflect on what I'd just witnessed.

At first glance, it looked like laziness or carelessness, but I don't think it was either. In a country where nearly, every aspect of life is tightly prescribed, maybe this was his way of carving out a tiny bit of personal freedom.

Somehow, for him, that was meaningful. It wasn't just convenience. It was control in the moment.

His message was clear, *"This rule doesn't make sense to me. If I must comply, I'll do it on my terms."*

I'd go on to tell this story to a few Chinese colleagues, genuinely curious to understand it better. One offered a brilliant insight.

She said, "That's called zuān kòngzi."
It means *"drilling into loopholes."*

She explained that while China emphasizes compliance and social harmony, it also breeds a strong culture of clever worka-rounds. It wasn't long into my moment of reflection that I joined Steven, and caught some z's of my own.

WILD CRAB AND KING LOUIS

On the approach to Wuxi, we perked up. We'd be heading straight to the factory before checking into the hotel. Surprisingly well-rested, Steven and I were ready to hit the ground running.

The factory owner was someone I'd known for years. This visit was partly to reinforce our existing business and partly to explore a new, adjacent product that his facility was well positioned to support.

We caught up a bit and mostly for Steven's benefit, we took a tour of the operation. It was more automated than most facilities I'd seen in China, impressively integrated, with metal stamping, fabrication, filling, and packaging all happening across a compact industrial campus under single ownership.

The owner went by Alex, but used "Lex" for short. I've always found the Western-facing names Chinese professionals choose for themselves intriguing. Often the meaning behind the name, the lore, the legacy, isn't fully known to them, yet it becomes part of their identity.

This Lex was no comic book villain, though he was certainly a formidable industrialist in his own right, well connected, deeply informed, and fully at home in Wuxi.

He had a depth of market insight and personal wisdom that earned my nickname for him, Mr. Law.

When I introduced him to Steven, he teased him lightly, without realizing the connection to his chosen name,

"Wow, Superman," he said.

It was a tip of the hat to his towering build, but also his gentle demeanor.

In the years to come, I grew to think of Steven as *Superman* too, for all the walls he crashed through to help us meet some truly tall orders.

We made our way to the Sofitel Hotel, just a short drive away. Lex would pick us up in a few hours for what he promised would be a crab extravaganza.

Once we got settled, we were hitting our stride. Mr. Law showed up, ready to represent.

"You and big man are in for treat," he said with a grin. First stop was the seafood market. That alone was an experience with rows of plastic bins, half-filled with sloshing water and very much alive, feisty crabs.

One of them had an eye fixed on freedom. "Big man" jumped back with the reflexes of someone who clearly had a basketball background. The vendor laughed. We all did.

Lex bargained like a true local, and we left with an enormous bag of crabs, tied off, still alive, and definitely kicking.

The best was yet to come.

Steven looked unsure, that same naughty crab seemed to have an eye on him from inside the mesh.

Lex led us to a familiar restaurant, and in we went. BYOC: Bring Your Own Crabs. Check.

What followed was part ritual, part necessity. The restaurant staff worked on steaming our army of crabs. Meanwhile, we were given the proper tools of the trade, bowls, plates, spoons, crab crackers, forks, all delivered sealed in tight plastic. A reasonably reassuring sign of cleanliness.

Then came the hot tea. Lex showed us the drill. We poured the piping hot tea into our bowls, swirled our chopsticks, spoons, and dishes in the scalding rinse, until we were certain that we were working with clean goods.

While the crabs steamed, snacks started arriving, including roasted peanuts, some finger foods, and a big bottle of Snow Beer, served with small glasses.

A toast was in order.

Lex lifted his glass, "To old friends and big appetites… may the claws to riches open wide and not cost us any fingers." *Ganbei!*

Just in time, the guests of honor arrived, our mountain of steamed mitten crabs, vivid orange shells glowing. We tied on our bibs and dove in.

It was a Snow storm of beer, hot steam rising from the table, an organized free-for-all as we cracked claws. No method to the madness, just us and the pile. Ginger and vinegar on standby.

There was, however, one moment of surgical precision. The real prize wasn't in the legs or claws. You cracked the top shell, and there it was, the golden roe, rich and savory. That's what all the buzz was about, and it lived up to the hype.

It felt like the final act had played. Bravos were in order. Not quite, indicated our host. The curtain had yet to fall. Lex wasn't finished. He had an encore in mind.

With the table now cleared, in came royalty.

Apparently, Lex had signaled the driver earlier to bring in a special treat, held back for just the right moment.

From a place that felt more crab shack than fine dining, emerged a bottle of none other than *Louis XIII*, the crown jewel of cognacs. And no, it wouldn't be poured into glass mugs with faded Snow Beer logos. Alongside the Baccarat crystal bottle were proper tulip-shaped crystal glasses, fitting companions for a spirit of such pedigree.

We were about to escalate our status, from cracked claws to noble notes. I wasn't exactly light on my feet after that much crab. Did that matter?

No. King Louis had summoned us, and duty called.

With grace and purpose, Lex poured our glasses, not a taste, a full pour. He was all in. So were we.

Steven, my young compadre, was about to experience a career moment far earlier than most. The big guy was in the right place at the right time.

Lex raised his glass, heart full,

"Here's not for what's to come, but for what we have."

The crystal clinked. We indulged. Conversation flowed. We talked families, life, and the deeper meanings behind our work. It was the perfect blend of friendship and business.

Back at the Sofitel, *fulfilled* would be an understatement.

The next two days in Wuxi would be a series of stops and visits, solving problems and managing tasks, but the moral of that night was clear, relationships matter.

Trust and loyalty are long-term currency in this business. Lex would get us out of a jam more than once in the years to come. And if things ever got tense, I'd just ask him, "What would Louis think?" We'd laugh, and somehow, the decision would make itself, just right.

The next morning, we boarded a Shenzhen Airlines flight to Zhuhai. A smooth flight, less than three hours.

A few years later, I'd get to know Zhuhai much more intimately, during the swine flu epidemic, as we relived together earlier.

For now, Steven and I headed to our go-to spot in town, the Holiday Inn. In my experience, it was the best place around. Over the years, I met plenty of fellow global sourcing road warriors there, from major European and U.S. shoe, furniture, and sunglasses brands, usually sharing a beer at the Blarney Stone Irish Pub adjacent to the lobby. *Water finds its own level.* In Zhuhai, for jet setters overseas, that meant the Holiday Inn.

The next day, we were scheduled to visit the head office of a supplier who specialized in fabricated metal and blown glass. We'd be reviewing design iterations for the upcoming catalog and discussing ways to consolidate some business.

Jamie, our lead contact, would pick us up at 9 a.m. Steven and I called it an early night.

LESSONS FROM QING DYNASTY

We started the next morning with breakfast, a Southern China buffet with standout dim sum. Jamie picked us up, and before long, we were at the office. Zhuhai is a coastal city surrounded by mountains and lined with palm trees. It's part of China's Greater Bay Area, an economic zone of rising significance.

As we walked through the factory's front office, one thing caught my eye, an aquarium. Inside were four long, silver fish, sleek and shiny. Jamie later told me they were *dragon fish*, revered for their wisdom and long lives. Some, depending on their bloodlines, could fetch tens of thousands of dollars.

We were brought into Mr. Xie's private office, a large space with leather couches and an ornate carved wood table. In the center sat a traditional Cantonese tea set.

Mr. Xie, in his 60s, had a calm-natured, deliberate demeanor. Though he spoke through a translator, he was zeroed in. This meeting would be as much about form as it was about function.

Naturally, we sat down for tea.

He began with a story. During the Qing Dynasty, he explained, an emperor would sometimes travel incognito among his people. On one such occasion, he visited a tea house and poured tea for his companion. The man, unable to kneel in gratitude, bent his index and middle fingers and tapped them on the table, a gesture symbolizing kneeling.

This became the origin of the *finger kowtow*, a tradition that lives on today, demonstrated by a couple of taps on the table when graciously receiving a cup of tea.

That morning was a masterclass in Cantonese tea tradition and enjoyment, and it had a lasting impression.

We spent the next two days reviewing over 100 product iterations. "Make this one taller." "Change that one to red." "Put this top on that base."

It was fun and creative. Jamie was a pro, sketching, noting details, keeping pace with our brainstorming. On our final night, we had a farewell dinner.

For all its industrial scale, Zhuhai was still at heart a fishing village, and Mr. Xie wanted to give us a proper sendoff.

At this kind of seafood restaurant, there are no menus. First, you walk past rows of tanks and pools to select your seafood. It's bagged, weighed, and sent to the kitchen. The dishes eventually rotate back to you on your table's Lazy Susan.

That night, I discovered my favorite dish in all of China, something I'd come to crave on future visits. It was called *Lobster Yee Mein*. We chose a New Zealand lobster from the tanks.

It came back baked, chopped into a deep dish over golden egg noodles in a creamy cheese sauce. It may sound like some kind of lobster mac and cheese, but erase that image. This was a whole lobster laid over rich, savory noodles. The sauce was pure magic.

We ate like ministers in the emperor's court Mr. Xie spoke about. After dinner, Steven and I said our goodbyes and expressed our thanks. The next morning, we'd be off again, bound for Dalian.

RUSSIAN BLUEPRINT

Our Air China flight into Dalian connected through Shanghai and took about seven hours.

Upon arrival, we made our way to another Shangri-La hotel, this one nestled in the heart of the city. Dalian wasn't a megametropolis like Shenzhen or Shanghai, but its role as a key logistics center and port city for Northeastern Asia made it no less important in terms of commerce and global trade.

Positioned on the Liaodong Peninsula, Dalian boasts year-round ice-free waters, a geographic advantage that hasn't gone unnoticed. Over a century earlier, Russia struck a deal with China to lease the area, aiming to develop a strategic seaport and commercial outpost.

As Steven and I approached our hotel, we passed clear imprints of that colonial past, neoclassical architecture, wide tree-lined boulevards, and a street grid that felt more St. Petersburg than China. It was an unexpected but fascinating blend of European design and Asian energy.

It's worth noting that just across the bay sits North Korea, a silent neighbor with a long-standing interest in Dalian's warm waters and unobstructed access to the sea.

This leg of the trip was focused on an ambiance products manufacturer, a newer supplier we'd met with a few times before. They were working on a collaborative design we planned to launch early the following year.

A snag had emerged in one of the production steps, and Steven was here to apply his technical wizardry to find a fix. I was there for support and make sure the solution, once found, stuck. We'd be heading to the factory first thing in the morning.

For now, we decided to get acquainted with Dalian.

After a chat with the hotel concierge, we took a pass on the more adventurous local offerings, grilled squid on a stick wasn't exactly what I had in mind for dinner, and instead found a Russian restaurant, a holdover from the city's unique history.

It was a cozy little spot with dark wood interiors and a nostalgic menu. We ordered beef stroganoff, which landed just right.

A small family band was playing live folk music, balalaika, accordion, and vocals, adding to the ambiance. The eldest daughter on the accordion seemed to have eyes for Steven. He, of course, was completely oblivious.

We went over our game plan for the next day and leaned back, soaking it all in.

The factory visit went smoother than expected. Steven was able to engineer a process tweak that solved the issue, that didn't happen every time, but when it did, it meant a total loss of an entire production batch.

I added value the best way I knew how, mainly enforcing that the SOP be updated to incorporate the improvement. Dalian ended up being a quick stop. Next up was Qingdao, to visit a supplier of metal kitchenware. Steven was excited about this one, and not just for the product line.

We managed to move up our flights, skipping the extra overnight in Dalian.

Shandong Airlines had a short hop available, just under an hour in the air, followed by a quick 30-minute drive into the city. We could have flown out in the morning, but in my experience, it's better to keep moving while the pace is good. It would be another Shangri-La, this time in Qingdao.

LEGACY ON TAP

Tomorrow was Friday, and the plan was to spend the day together on supplier visits. After that, Steven and I would part ways. Something had come up at a factory in Saigon that required my attention over the weekend, while Steven would stay on in Qingdao, mixing business with a little well-earned pleasure.

He had his sights set on the Qingdao Brewery. I'd toured it before and knew he was in for something special.

Here's an interesting nuance, the city of Qingdao is pronounced "Ching-dao," with emphasis on the "ch" sound, so naturally, you'd think the beer, named after the city, would follow suit. Thanks to early international branding falling victim to a pre-pinyin anomaly, the name stuck as Tsingtao, and the pronunciation morphed into the now widely accepted "Sing-tao."

Mispronunciation aside, Tsingtao remains China's most internationally recognized beer, and for good reason.

Originally established by German brewers in 1903, it benefited from their strict adherence to Reinheitsgebot purity laws and centuries of brewing tradition. Then came the Japanese occupation, bringing new efficiencies, equipment upgrades, and scaled production. The result? A beer with a rich, layered heritage. Unfortunately, I wouldn't be sharing a cold brew with Steven this time.

BATTLE PLANS OVER BOLOGNESE

Reaching Vietnam was easy enough, via China Eastern Airlines. With a short connection in Shanghai, total travel time was just about seven hours. I was on the ground by midafternoon.

After checking into the Hotel Continental, I had a dinner meeting arranged with members of the factory's management team to discuss weekend plans and how we'd address the issues at hand. We were behind schedule, and there was a seasonal push to get back on track and avoid disruption to the supply chain.

There was a rare gem on the property, an Italian restaurant called *Venezia*. The Hotel Continental itself had a storied past. During the Vietnam War, it had served as a hub for war correspondents and diplomats, affectionately nicknamed the "Continental Shelf" for the outdoor terrace where press briefings and informal gatherings took place.

Tonight, Venezia would serve as our war room to go over how we were going to deal with some not-so-great news of our own.

Over the next two days, the team came together. We managed to identify a combination of root causes that had been slowing the flow of goods, some related to logistics, others to production bottlenecks.

With a few strategic adjustments and creative process refinements, we were able to solve the issues.

By Monday, we'd established a steady cadence, confident we could meet seasonal demand without missing a beat at retail. Fortunately, the problems had been flagged early, and corrective actions implemented just in time to get in front of anything more damaging.

SIZE MATTERS

The owner, a Vietnamese national who lived abroad, flew in and visited the factory on Sunday to check on progress and ensure I had the support needed.

It was a good opportunity for us to catch up. The way we did turned out to be unusual, but it became a priceless experience I'll never forget.

The factory was about a three-hour drive from the Hotel Continental. I had been picked up by a company car on arrival, but Vu, the owner, drove himself in.

He arrived behind the wheel of a shiny black Buick Regal GS, a status symbol in Vietnam at the time. Pricey to import and punching beyond its weight, it made a statement.

In a playful spirit, and he'd quickly regret it,

Vu tossed me the keys and said,

"Want to drive us back?"

"Sure," I said, without hesitation.

Vu was surprised by my reaction, but went along with it.

It was in his nature to flash a little style now and then, and today, he was feeling bold. Luckily for me, we weren't in Malaysia or Hong Kong, where the steering wheel is on the right side. That would've been one too many adjustments, especially considering the landscape I was about to navigate.

Before I could start the engine,

Vu leaned over.

"Let me give you the lay of the land," he said, "so we don't cause an international incident."

By all appearances, Vu looked like a longtime subscriber to *GQ*. His thick, sculpted black hair barely moved, even in the heat.

This day, he wore a bright polo with the collar popped and enough charm to pull it off, barely. I half-joked to myself that, younger, he could've passed for Dustin Nguyen in his *21 Jump Street* days.

With his signature flair and self-assurance, Vu leaned back in the passenger seat and began,

"Jarrod, you need to remember one thing, there are big fish and small fish. Bicycles, scooters, pedestrians... they're the small fish. In this car, *you* are the big fish." I nodded.

"As the big fish, you must swim gently through the current. The small fish will part for you, naturally."

He paused. "But," he added, holding up a finger, "just like in life... there's always a bigger fish than you. If you see a freight truck or bus, you are now the small fish. Adjust accordingly."

"Got it," I said. He nodded, reassured.

"Let's go, Big Fish. Take it slow."

We had an edge-of-the-seat three-hour drive ahead of us, and once I was behind the wheel, I had no intention of giving it up.

For the first hour, it was smooth countryside driving. I'd seen the scenery before from the passenger seat, water buffalo grazing, rice paddies glistening, a flat expanse of swampy green that offered a charming view of the South Vietnamese terrain.

Then we entered a city and came upon our first lighted intersection. It was exactly what Vu had prepared me for, a fisherman's paradise. Vendors pushed carts across traffic. Scooters weaved in every direction. Bicycles toted stacked packages.

A couple of trucks rumbled past, indifferent to the concept of lanes. I eased in slowly, and as promised, the *small fish*, shoulder to shoulder, unpanicked, shifted like a living tide adjusting to the slow arrival of deeper water. The trucks stayed in their lane, too. Professionals, I thought.

One of the truck drivers looked over and did a double-take. I must have been a sight, a foreigner behind the wheel this far out of downtown was not something you saw every day.

After a few more intersections and another hour or so of navigating through semi-urban entanglement, we hit the high seas, the center of Saigon. As we approached the Hotel Continental, the density of scooters, bicycles, and pedestrians formed a living current. By then, I'd more than been around the block. I had the confidence of a local.

We arrived safe and sound. The look of relief on Vu's face was priceless. I was all smiles, feeling accomplished, maybe even deserving of a Vietnamese driver's license. At least, the *GQ* subscription. Of course, that would be the one and only time I'd ever drive in the country. Once was enough. I checked it off the bucket list.

SONG OF THE FARMER

During the remainder of that year, Steven fully stepped into his role, allowing us to mostly divide and conquer.

The ground game we initiated in Shanghai had proven to be a sound decision. Item by item, product line by product line, factory by factory, we transitioned to offshore and factory-direct sources. The results would have a significant impact on our bottom line for years to come, establishing competitive advantages that became a platform for long-term growth.

One of the most important lessons I took from this pivotal period in my career was none of it was guaranteed. The outcomes didn't happen by accident, nor by luck.

In fact, there were more than a few jump scares, moments that could have derailed the entire project. Any good fortune we had was from what has since become my personal formula for global trade, a formula I continue to refine.

That recipe starts with the belief that open minds close the best deals. I learned to listen more than I spoke, genuinely curious about what others had to say. Most of the time, their answers came before the questions even needed to be asked. I came to live by the principle that taking an unfair advantage today almost always turns into a greater disadvantage tomorrow. I found that the most mean-ingful insights often came when I wasn't looking, and from the unlikeliest of sources, so I pay attention. I made a point to slow down and take in the details, to taste the fruits, smell the roses, and study my surroundings with a passion for learning. When things went wrong, I made it a practice to first point out what went right. Even as a leader, I was led by the belief that all business is local, and always between people, not just entities. That meant getting to know the people behind the products just as much as the products themselves. In the end, what drives me now, is the sense that there's no end. It's always unfinished business.

I share these takeaways in the hope they may resonate with you, to embrace and refine in your own way. For me, they've led to lifelong friendships just as much as phenomenal business results. Worth keeping in mind, the relationships will outlast any praise for a job well done.

All that said, I encourage you to take the microphone and sing your ballad. Grab the keys if they're tossed your way. If you're able, raise your glass, it may not be Louis XIII, but it'll taste just as incredible in good company.

At the same time, if I may offer one last belief, one that took a while to learn. Don't rush it. I've found that when I hurried to be first, I rarely was. The cheese, so to speak, always moved farther away. When I was deliberate, swift, but not hasty, the reward ended up in my hands instead of slipping through my fingers.

Over time, I learned to embrace the way of the farmer and the fisherman, not the fry cook.

6

GUT, CHECKED:
FELT BEFORE PROVEN

At the outset of this journey, I spoke about the importance of developing your instincts, how they become the real differentiator when the rules don't fit the moment and the data comes up short. However, instincts don't arrive fully formed. They're earned over time, forged by fire, shaped through exposure, sharpened by missteps, and tested when the stakes are high. We now explore the proving ground where those instincts are put to work, where a sixth sense surfaces between the numbers and the noise. Sometimes it's a gut check. Other times it's a deliberate voice saying, "this doesn't feel right," even when the spreadsheet says go. From the unshakable feeling that something's off to the moments when certainty comes before evidence, these are the lessons you can't always explain, but you ignore them at your peril. The stories here live in that space between logic and inner voice, between the lines, where leaders are made not just by what they know, but by what moves from within.

If I were to describe how my own instincts became sharply defined, how exactly did that "sixth sense" happen? How did the moments, missteps, and insights I've shared throughout this book contribute to what I now consider my professional superpower?

Let's get into it.

First, let's be clear. Instinct can mean different things to different people. I'm not referring to impulses or emotion-driven intuition. What I'm talking about are *learned instincts*, the kind that are built over time through repetition, reflection, and deliberate processing of experience.

They form an internal compass, one that guides your actions based not on guesswork, but on *lived knowledge*. It's the inner voice that whispers truths you can't yet explain, but somehow know.

These instincts are fed by a personal database of exposure, sharpened through both intake and analysis, forged by fire one might say.

PROVING GROUND

Let's take the experience I had on the road to Wuxi. A few minutes into the drive, the seatbelt warning chimed, *ding, ding, ding.* I looked back. My colleague was buckled in and fast asleep. The driver, however, was not. Instead, he reached for a small chrome tongue, a trick gadget used to silence the alarm without actually fastening the belt.

At first glance, I could've disregarded it as a one-off workaround. Instead, instinct told me to dig deeper. Why was this considered normal? Why go to such lengths to avoid a simple safety measure? That moment wasn't just about observing the trick, it was about processing what it *meant*.

What it revealed were underlying cultural and political signals, how compliance might be enforced on paper but sidestepped in practice. That realization got filed away.

Later on, when I came across a supplier who insisted their quality protocols were airtight, only for inspections to reveal cracks, my gut was already primed. A workaround was likely in play.

That gave me a place to start looking.

Another example, in Vietnam, when we were collecting candle quotes from multiple factories, the numbers varied for most items, except one, the tea light.

Every single factory quoted the exact same price.

That didn't make sense. Not at first glance.

Instead of accusing anyone, we followed the nudging alarm our instincts set off. It felt like someone else, a shared source, was behind those numbers. Sure enough, we traced it back to a mystery factory they were all sourcing from.

We didn't see a red flag. We *felt* one.

Then there was the visit to a candle factory in Bangalore. From the moment we pulled up, the surroundings told a story, of a collapsed gate, tangled power lines, a concrete shell of a building.

We'd seen setups like this before.

Our instincts weren't triggered by aesthetics. They were triggered by what such conditions *usually meant*. We didn't know where the quality problem would be yet, but we knew there'd likely be one. We found it, deep in the wax room.

Contrast that with the presentation I gave to a major petroleum company in Saudi Arabia. No one jumped to their feet in applause, but I walked out knowing it had gone well.

How? Subtle markers, a senior executive offering encouraging remarks, the meeting going over time without anyone checking their watch, and specific questions that went *beyond* the presentation, into implementation.

My internal database flagged all of it. My instinct told me this followed the same dynamic as other meetings that led to green lights.

LEARNED INSTINCTS

Let's remember back to our encounter in Da Nang, with Huy and the three watchful dogs. It was still early in our discussions, long before pricing or terms were even on the table, when Huy made a passing comment that stuck with us.

We've been burned before, he said,

referencing a prior buyer who'd promised large orders but never followed through, leaving him holding the bag, thousands of dollars in unsold inventory.

That wasn't just a throwaway remark.

It deserved more thought, a mental note taken for later. He hadn't framed it as a warning, but our instinct heard it as one. Not a red flag exactly, but more of a caution sign, subtle, yet significant. We hadn't asked for extended payment terms yet, but we knew that when we did, it would strike the same nerve, the risk of fronting inventory without a guarantee. To be fair, he didn't know us.

We hadn't earned his trust.

That early signal gave us space, not to respond immediately, but to prepare. When the time came, Chad was ready.

He laid out a compelling case, showing how our volume forecast and early concessions could make the arrangement both secure and worthwhile. It wasn't just persuasive. It was preemptive.

Instinct isn't always about reacting in the moment.

Sometimes, it's knowing that a moment is coming.

How about a fun, more widely practical example?

The three-hour drive back from the factory to downtown Saigon wasn't just a return trip, it was a lesson. Not in logistics, not in manufacturing, but in movement.

During the drive, Vu offered wisdom as the road unfolded in front of us like a test.

"Big fish go slow," he said, nodding toward a truck ahead.

"Small fish… they move fast." Scooters darted in and out like minnows, weaving between trucks, taxis, bicycles, and food carts. There were no lanes, no signals, just a shared instinct.

It would've been easy to misread the whole scene as anarchy. It wasn't. It was choreography. No horns. No shouting. Just a system built on awareness and a jazzy sense of syncopated movement. One thing was clear. You couldn't charge through it like a bull in a china shop and expect it to work out.

Instead, I followed my gut, slow, steady, predictable.

Awkward and unsure at first, but soon, something clicked. As long as I respected the flow, I didn't disrupt it. Others adjusted naturally. No drama. I realized the space I was being granted wasn't a matter of right, it was a matter of rhythmic surprise.

That's the thing about instincts. You don't get them from a manual. You earn them by paying attention, by knowing when to move, when to pause, and when to stay in your lane.

Smooth journeys aren't accidents. They're the product of decisions, timed just right.

CAN'T FLIGHT THIS FEELING

You might be wondering, why emphasize instincts at all? Doesn't that put feelings above data? Not at all. Instincts and data aren't opposites, they're collaborators.

In fact, instincts often guide what data to collect, or which conditions to apply in interpreting it.

They accelerate decision-making in ambiguity.

They steer you toward the right questions *before* a problem becomes visible. Instincts let you see what others miss. You detect patterns and anomalies that don't show up in spreadsheets or executive summaries.

They help you act faster when clarity is lacking.

In fast-moving environments, instincts enable confident decisions without over-analysis.

They raise alarms.

When something feels off, even if you can't explain it yet, instincts buy you time and awareness.

They adapt across cultures.

In global business, instincts help you recognize unspoken rules, shifting power dynamics, and subtle signs of respect or risk.

Sharpened, they unlock hidden opportunities.

The broader your exposure, and the more your experiences are processed, not just survived, the stronger your ability to anticipate problems and capitalize on what's beneath the surface.

BETWEEN THE LINES

There's a wealth of writing out there about learning instincts, intuition, decision theory, and behavioral psychology, the many ways we perceive, process, and act on information.

I've only touched on instincts here in broad strokes. My goal isn't to lecture, which would be overreaching for me, but to leave the finer points to the scholars. My intent is to show how instinct plays a defining role in global business, with all its layers, complexities, and cultural nuance. I've leaned on my instincts more times than I can count,

to see what's between the lines,

to sense what's coming around the corner,

to decide what not to say,

to recognize when a door that looks closed might actually be cracked open.

Gut, Checked

If that internal whisper becomes a little louder for you after reading this, then we'll have found the same frequency

7

TERMINAL INSIGHTS:
A GATE TO WHAT COMES NEXT

Every journey comes with a layover, the moment you pause, reflect, and prepare for what's next. Mine has taken me through factory floors and policy shifts, across cultures and continents, with just enough turbulence to make it interesting. These final thoughts aren't simply wrap-up, they're launchpads. As one lands, another is cleared for takeoff. Whether it's a new market, a different lens, or simply a new approach, the next opportunity is already boarding. There's no assigned seat, but for those who board with purpose, the runway is wide open. By the time your flight lifts off, one truth is undeniable, trade isn't only global, it's personal. What you bring home isn't just product, price, or terms. It's insight. It's perspective. It's the difference you make... and the advantage you carry forward.

GREAT WALL OF TARIFFS

Beginning with Donald Trump's first presidential term, importers were certainly well versed in how duties were calculated, even antidumping and countervailing ones, but tariffs, not as much.

Surely the term rang a bell. Maybe from that foggy memory of a high school history class, where the Smoot-Hawley Tariff Act got mentioned in a chapter on the Great Depression. Something about trying to help farmers and manufactures, but triggering economic quagmire instead.

The seasoned importer might recall Reagan's more targeted move in the '80's, including a tariff on heavyweight motorcycles to give Harley-Davidson relief from a wave of Japanese imports, and tariff on Japanese electronics in retaliation for a failed semiconductor deal. The astute colleague might even correct you at lunch and remind you it was actually George W. Bush, not Trump, who was the first president of the 21st century to slap tariffs on steel.

However, even among the best-informed professionals back then, you wouldn't hear many talking in *section numbers* of the Trade Act of 1974 and the Trade Expansion Act of 1962.

Today if you're in supply chain or a related field chances are good when talking with peers someone will blame their anguish, anxiety or urgency on Section 201, 232 or 301.

Thanks to Trump, even tariff veterans were humbled by the unfamiliarity of the International Emergency Economic Powers Act of 1977, affectionately referred to as "IEEPA."

Trying to figure it all out, so that it could be explained to others in the organization, all asking the same questions, the conversation at one point sounded something like this:

"So, the steel tariff stacks with what you're calling the 'fentanyl tariff,' but only from China? What do you mean it's a derivative, so it's 50% more…Is that like de minimis? Remind me, who's 'reciprocating' and who's 'retaliating?' When's the effective date? …is that when it gets here or when it ships? What is Vietnam's rate, 46%? Or, is that Thailand's? Oh, they're both 10% now… until when? And tell me, for the love of Pete—what stacks?!"

Abbot and Costello would've had a field day. These tariffs are sketch-comedy gold. So where do we go from here? Is there light at the end of the tunnel, or is that the headlight of a freight train heading straight for us.

Hard to say. One thing's for sure; we're going to be in this tunnel a while. As we take steps toward a clearer path, it's worth revisiting the 3P concept introduced earlier, a practical approach for navigating pressure while reaching for innovation. It's the idea of protecting, piloting, and patching the supply chain, holding the line on current needs while testing what's next.

Let's set the stage. The earlier Trump tariffs, back in 2018-2019, rolled out essentially in four lists, running the trap line on Chinese goods. There was structure back then. Tariff rates generally fell between 7.5% and 25%, the scope was mainly limited to China, and there was even a pathway for exemption if U.S.-based sourcing wasn't feasible. Sounds reasonable, right?

Better still, when one importer successfully argued for an exemption, that lifeline applied to all, anyone bringing in the same product could benefit. Small-value shipments often flew under the radar entirely, thanks to the *de minimis* rule, which spared American small businesses, especially online sellers on platforms like eBay and Amazon, from being caught in a tariff's snare.

If you were operating inside a Foreign Trade Zone (FTZ), there were legitimate workarounds. When the manufacturing process inside the zone altered the product enough to avoid tariff coverage, you could avoid the tariff duty altogether. Even without an FTZ, you could drawback tariff-duties if goods were re-exported.

Finally, there was a clear process and reasonably fair level of transparency. Not without stakeholder challenges to the process and authority behind the tariff actions. However, in retrospect, there was at least some oxygen left in the room. Before tariffs were imposed, the U.S. Trade Representative (USTR) held public hearings where importers could present their case.

This gave stakeholders the opportunity to raise fact-based concerns before the tariffs took effect. That meant formulating a strategy could begin before impact was felt.

Now, contrast that with the tariffs imposed in 2025. Hold tight, we're about to ride the *Harmonized System* straight off the rails. Even my driver back in Wuxi would've strapped in for this one. The wheel-popping, curb-hopping rickshaw racer in Bangalore? He'd trade his ballcap for a helmet.

What came next wasn't just a policy shift, it was a tariff *earthquake*. The epicenter? 1600 Pennsylvania Avenue, but the tremors would be felt all the way to Ulaanbaatar, Mongolia.

After the quake came the *tsunami of uncertainty…* and anxiety. The quake had a name, "IEEPA." It packed a punch, invoking national security concerns tied to the illegal fentanyl drug trade and critical foreign-made resources.

Were there stakeholder hearings? Nope.

This roller coaster started at the very moment before it made its colossal downward spiral at break-neck speeds, through corkscrews and loops, forwards and backwards. Naturally, nausea occurred, in the form of global trading disorder.

Just when you thought the ride was over, you'd find yourself right back in line, for another go at the thrill ride of a lifetime.

Let's talk about some of those twists and turns. *De minimis*? Gone. FTZ advantages? Severely limited. Goods entered the zone in "privileged status," meaning what came in most cases had to go out the same way. Drawbacks? Also diminished. Exemptions for unavailable U.S. goods? Forget it. Well, mostly, some exemptions, in certain categories of goods, were carved out, for a limited time as they underwent further investigation and assessment.

Was this tariff a loner? Not even close. It stacked right on top of earlier ones and those that followed, including the ones all of the way back in 2018.

The kicker? The part we'd all rush to post about, like some heart-throbbing theme park experience. The tariff rate today could change tomorrow… then again, the next day… and again after that. No warning. No pattern. Just whiplash.

This ride didn't say

"keep your arms inside." It said,

"put your hands up and close your eyes."

There's more.

Under normal circumstances, the administrative chain of events follows a well-established process. First, the President or USTR announces that a tariff decision has been made.

That announcement typically comes in the form of an Executive Order or Presidential Proclamation, either delivered with ceremony from the podium or Oval Office, as President Trump prefers, or low-key uploaded online for us trade nerds to gleefully hunt down.

A few days later, the official details land in the Federal Register, the real home of fine print. That's where subject-matter experts in supply chain management and trade compliance go to confirm what's actually happening.

The Federal Register typically includes an effective date far enough out to let importers take a collective breath, before havoc-mitigating actions are put in play.

Back to the *IEEPA earthquake*. At first, it seemed to follow the usual pattern. Then something unprecedented happened. The effective dates? So short, they were almost immediate. Importers barely had time to react.

Suddenly, the Executive Order or Proclamation became the only place to track what was coming next. Sometimes even, the White House Fact Sheet that preceded those published documents, was the only source available in time to react.

Then, the real fun began. Announcements weren't just coming from the White House podium, official website posting, or press briefings. They were dropping directly from the President's *Truth Social* account.

Yes, global trade policy, with worldwide economic implications, impacting virtually every U.S. importer and foreign exporter overnight, was being initially broadcast via social media. In many cases, these posts didn't even contain enough detail to decipher how they'd officially land. Reportedly, foreign trade ministers at times were left scratching their heads, unsure if or how the coming policies announced applied to their country.

With all the obstacles out there, it can feel like there's no safe harbor, no good options. Just throw our hands in the air, scream on the way down, and go along for the ride? No chance.

That's not supply chain management, and it's not what the business needs. As the saying goes, and we've all heard it, "If it were easy, everyone would be doing it."

How do we chart a course in the dark? We shine some light using our proven three-step approach, Protect, Pilot, and Patch. As my favorite consultant used to say, let's put some meat on the bones.

It makes sense to start by protecting what we have. That means asking, what can we do right now to mitigate the impact of tariffs? At first glance, maybe it's shifting supply here, then there, then back to where we started, before moving it again. That might work, at least in the short term, assuming we're not locked into molds, tooling, or other long-lead-time factors.

Hopefully, we are in a position to leverage our resilient supply chain with built-in supply backups.

Truth is, in this kind of tariff environment, completely avoiding increased costs isn't likely. Not impossible, but each product comes with its own quirks. More often, we're trying to soften the blow, not expecting to dodge it entirely.

What follows isn't a one-size-fits-all solution. That would be overly ambitious, and unrealistic.

The point here is to demonstrate a *framework*, one you can adapt based on your products, your origins, your risk exposure. Some examples of "protect" moves might include, bypassing the U.S. entirely on certain international orders and importing directly into the destination country, structuring transactions under the "first sale" rule to reduce dutiable value, diversifying supply to a comparable, lower-cost source that maintains quality and service, leveraging a Foreign Trade Zone (FTZ) for cash flow advantages, and negotiating pricing concessions from factories to share in the tariff burden, while keeping Customs valuation compliance airtight.

Once you're doing all you can to protect the business from short-term damage, the question becomes, *what are you doing to pilot toward something better,* foreseeably, longer-term?

Maybe your product is currently made in China and you're exploring a shift to Mexico, where the USMCA eliminates the tariff burden. Maybe your item's classified under an HTS code that falls under Section 232 tariffs due to its steel or aluminum content, and you're looking into alternative materials to change the classification entirely. Whatever the case, these long-term solutions shouldn't wait. They should run in parallel with your short-term defenses.

Now let's throw one more ball into the air, *Patch*. This is the bridge, the practical work that connects today's reality with tomorrow's vision.

Say you want to shift final assembly to Mexico, but a key subassembly still depends on capabilities only available in China, specialized equipment, advanced skills, or both. You've identified a couple options which include, setting up automation back in the U.S. to re-shore and handle it yourself or helping your Mexican supplier upgrade to handle both subassembly and final manufacturing. Whatever the case, your supply chain is now firing on all cylinders, protecting today, piloting tomorrow, and patching the gap in between.

There's no doubt that navigating tariffs and geopolitics while building for the future is tough work. Especially when the rules keep changing. With a data-driven mindset, cross-functional collaboration, and some outside expertise where it helps, real solutions emerge.

From there, it's about staying focused, aligned, and ready to adjust. Expect that you *will* get curveballs. Maybe mid-plan, maybe right at the finish line. If that happens, go back to your 3P map and reroute. The process is flexible, and it works.

FACE THE DIFFERENCE

When I look back on all the trips abroad, I'm struck by a deep sense of gratitude.

Work took me on more than a hundred journeys across dozens of countries and multiple continents, amounting to the equivalent of years spent in foreign lands.

I had the opportunity to be hands-on in ways most careers never allow. In between factory visits and business meetings, I managed to witness some of the world's wonders, along with a few hidden gems.

Along the way, I made friendships that outlasted the projects themselves. The global sourcing ventures I've led over the years delivered outcomes I'm proud of.

While I haven't shared every story in these pages, I've included a few adventures and mishaps that offer a window into how the unfamiliar became training ground to develop my learned instincts. Over the years, I've refined how best to protect the business from threats, pilot innovation that turns weakness into new strengths and the patchwork to realize fully developed opportunities.

One of the biggest lessons of all for me has been the discovery that at the end of every big project or journey, it comes down to the people involved, whose efforts and choices shape every outcome.

That reminds me of something I've learned to value more and more over the years, the idea of *face*. Face isn't just a Chinese cultural framework, it's rooted in universal human behavior, as I've come to see it. In China, it's especially important in business. It plays out in ways that can feel very different if you're used to American corporate culture.

There are really two sides to *face*.

One is *saving face*, being mindful of how you give feedback, especially not shaming someone in front of others, calling them out, or making them feel small.

It's not about avoiding accountability.

It's about preserving relationships and showing respect, even in tough conversations.

For example, instead of saying, "that won't work," you might say, "That could be difficult." Instead of, "How did you mess this up…" or, "you failed," you can say, "This was a tough one. We missed the mark. How do we fix it and make sure it doesn't happen again?" It's still honest, but it's collaborative. The tone matters.

It's not about finger-pointing, it's about solving problems together. The old saying applies, you attract more with honey than vinegar.

If you're coming from a typical American business background, this might feel overly cautious, or even soft.

We're used to direct feedback. "Own it. Fix it. Move on." There's nothing inherently wrong with that but if you're working in a global setting, or especially in China, what works at home can fall flat, or worse, cause real damage. If the goal is to actually resolve issues and keep moving forward, it's better to tune into the cultural dynamics at play.

It's not about being less honest.

It's about being more effective. *Saving face* has real strategic value in business, but there's another side to it that's just as powerful, and honestly, not used enough.

This is referred to as *giving face*.

Giving face means publicly showing respect, whether it's toward someone's rank, contribution, or effort. It could be as simple as giving a shout-out in a meeting for a job well done. You're putting a spotlight on someone, not for show, but because it's earned. That moment of recognition? It changes how they see themselves.

While we tend to talk about *face* in the context of Chinese culture, it's also deeply embedded in many other parts of Asia, including Japan, South Korea, Vietnam, Thailand, just to name a few. These are relationship-first cultures. Honor and respect aren't just gestures, they're currency.

This ties directly into another business talking point we love to throw around, *collaboration.*

Everyone claims they're collaborative. It's on the slide deck. It's in the values statement. However, if we're being honest, real collaboration only shows up in how well we listen, how respectfully we communicate, and how we treat each other in the tough moments. If you want authentic collaboration, thinking in terms of *face* can help get you there.

That means being tactful, encouraging and transparent. Yes, transparent. It means inviting people to be a part of the mission, not just assigned tasks.

You'll know you're getting it right when team members don't just raise a red flag after something's gone wrong, or worse, lack the confidence to raise it at all. Instead, they come to you early, with the problem and a couple of possible fixes.

That's a whole different level of engagement. That's someone who feels ownership. Usually, it starts with how they're treated when they speak up, whether they're made to feel small, or whether they're given *face*.

That's really the bigger picture, because how people feel in those moments says everything about the kind of leader you are, and the kind of culture you're building.

SUPPORTING CAST

Now that we're focused on being better versions of ourselves, ever-attentive and mindful of our interactions with people, there's another impactful way to put those skills and newly refined charisma to good use.

Throughout these stories, a common thread emerged.

A supporting cast.

Remember Wei Bo in Malaysia, and Jason in Korea?

You might wonder, what form did the casting call take to find these star performers who ended up opening doors, making critical introductions, and transferring key relationships?

Without Jason, I wouldn't have had the opportunity for that cup of coffee in Shanghai, with the Korean *ninja*, Min Jae, on my own at that point. There probably wouldn't have been the required trust or interest for that meeting.

It's something worth remembering, though often not realized early enough, *buying* is equal parts, or more, *selling*.

You're selling the opportunity to partner for supply, which means you're putting forward your company, your products, and your reputation in the marketplace. More than anything, you're selling yourself. Persuading others to trust you. To take you seriously. To ultimately respect you.

Essentially, you're answering a silent question, which is, *are you worth the time and effort to get to know?*

That has to happen before you can close any deal.

There's a lot to unpack here, and I'm focusing on just one piece of the toolkit. Let's call it networking.

However, a word of caution, in a broader sense. Think back to Min Jae and our business card exchange. Was it more form than substance? Relationships develop over time, and they're on shaky ground in the beginning. You could work hard and earn your seat at the table, only to offend or put off the person across from you, defeating the purpose and wasting everyone's time.

It's something to stay mindful of, always.

Let's talk about building your team. Generally speaking, we all know how this works. When we're younger, it happened more naturally. I remember countless times when I had a friend who had another friend, and before long, we were all close friends.

Relationships transfer. They multiply. They grow. Before you know it, you've got a full cast of familiar characters. It's not only a fortunate position to be in for your professional life, but a richly rewarding one in so many other ways.

Where to start? Maybe you're newly entering the profession. In my opinion, that's an even better reason to invest early in your professional network. This was the time for me.

My first step was full immersion into professional organizations, like-minded stakeholders from all aspects of the industry and at varying levels of experience.

There were other members like me, wide-eyed and full of untested ideas. Also, in the room, there were seasoned veterans to learn from. I joined the Council of Supply Chain Management Professionals (CSCMP). Back then, it was called the Council of Logistics Management (CLM).

I became active in industry clubs, fraternal organizations, and professional associations more aligned with steering the industry at large. I also engaged with specialized supply chain-facing groups that offered a narrow lens into particular sectors of the profession, such as logistics law and international trade.

This was a voluntary endeavor. My employers during that time weren't pushing me to do it. There was general support, but not nearly the same level of encouragement to engage the broader industry as there is today, unless, of course, you were in sales. In that case, by all means, companies were behind you joining every peer group that happened to double as a target-rich environment.

Nothing wrong with that, by the way. It pays to connect with all types of stakeholders.

I learned something early that stuck with me. A mentor once put it simply… *When asked to be involved, say yes.*

If you show up and participate in these peer groups, and again, use that charm of yours, eventually, the more influential members of the group will take notice. It might pull you out of your comfort zone, but it's well worth it. You could be asked to join a council, committee, task group, or help coordinate an event.

For me, the answer was *yes*, every time.

That led to experiences and relationships, friendships, even, that became the foundation of my professional network.

Back then, it was a powerful Rolodex. In today's terms, I was beginning to be Linked-In.

Within five years, my reputation as a "yes man" had elevated my status and access far beyond what I expected. Somehow, I found the time to serve on the Logistics Committee of the Transportation Lawyers Association, as a board director for the Los Angeles Transportation Club, a board director for the Citrus Belt Traffic Club, and to rise through the ranks of CLM to become Vice President of Programs for the Southern California Roundtable, which included a leadership role for its annual symposium in partnership with USC's Marshall School of Business.

More often than not, I've found that members of these organizations participate from a distance, maybe attending an annual conference once a year.

Don't get me wrong, those conferences are great, and a lot of resources are remotely accessible and valuable. CSCMP's EDGE annual conference and expo is a must for any practitioner who wants to keep a finger on the pulse of the industry.

For me, the greater value was found behind the scenes, working in concert with others. Remember that gentle pull out of your comfort zone? There were other benefits to this level of professional interaction, even beyond the priceless relationships with peers turned close colleagues or friends.

Public speaking didn't come naturally to me. I had a lot to say, but not exactly the confidence, or the artful delivery, to share those thoughts and ideas effectively. That was both a weakness and an opportunity.

Getting involved at a deeper level with these professional organizations helped me overcome that and seize the chance to grow. It was a supportive environment that exposed me to board-room dynamics, event planning, public relations, marketing, membership services, and yes, even some time holding the microphone or standing at the podium.

I am counting those times calling out raffle tickets.

Another avenue I pursued early, and continue to this day, was engaging with governments.

One valuable event that comes to mind was a business delegation I joined with the City of Ontario, California. The mayor of Ontario had organized an official trip to China, where we met with several mayors from cities including Shenzhen, Dongguan, Guangzhou, and a few others.

The intent was a mayor-to-mayor leadership venue that ultimately connected business delegates from both sides of the Pacific. At the same time, each Chinese mayor had the opportunity to showcase their city, highlighting development projects, competitive advantages, and why their municipality was ideal for commercial activity and investment.

Ontario, California, is located about 50 miles from the Port of Los Angeles / Long Beach, which together make up the largest port complex in the United States by a wide margin.

Well-positioned geographically, Ontario serves as a logistics nucleus and strategic inland hub for goods arriving from Asia. It plays a critical role in processing imports, whether across docks, over rails, through its international airport, or via interstates connecting the West and East coasts.

During that trip, I met half a dozen strong contacts who helped me better understand the business landscape in China. Some coached me on how to find reliable intel to research supply capabilities and resources. I provided the same in return as it related to trading corridors into the U.S., such as Ontario.

A couple of those contacts turned out to be close allies for years to come.

A more targeted approach to networking came from my growing interest in Malaysia, particularly in fuel products, but others as well. This turned out to be a fun experience.

There was a dinner organized by the Consulate General of Malaysia in Los Angeles, a business outreach event similar in spirit to the Ontario delegation, but in this case, everyone was under one roof, and fortunately for me, it was stateside.

Several Malaysian delegates, much like our Ontario group earlier, had made the trans-Pacific journey.

Let's return to that earlier point about form and substance. The dinner was designed to be festive. Wearing a *batik shirt* was recommended. These are the familiar floral or geometric patterned silk-like shirts that stand out at social occasions in Malaysia, including both business and government functions.

The Consulate General was hoping to introduce a touch of national culture as a way to make the evening memorable and meaningful. Now, no one was required to wear batik for entry. I could've worn the tried-and-true navy-blue suit and tie, maybe dressed it up with a floral accent to meet the festivities halfway.

Yet, the request was made, and this *yes-man* was all in. This was pre-Amazon days, which meant physically shopping for an authentic batik shirt in Los Angeles. I didn't choose the boldest one in the store, but I'll admit, it was on the louder side of the spectrum.

My choice was a batik with a deep navy base, orange hibiscus blooms and gold swirls that gave it pop. My good friend Vu back in Saigon, with all of his *GQ* style, would have approved.

Untucked and wearing my opening remarks,

I showed up to the dinner, ready to mingle. The experience was more than worthwhile. The contacts I made that night helped unlock what had previously been a distant and unfamiliar landscape, eventually leading me to meet Wei Bo.

To my surprise, most attendees who weren't from Malaysia chose a more conservative route. That's fine, of course. If tasteful and appropriate, standing out, being noticed, showing some charisma, can pay off in the end.

Thinking back to those annual conferences for large organizations like CSCMP's EDGE, I found them to be packed with peer interactions, breakout sessions, keynote addresses, and social events that were extremely valuable. On the lighter side, I remember one in particular where Bob Eubanks recounted highlights from decades of hosting *The Newlywed Game*, an endless catalog of comedy.

However, for me, the greater value came from tighter-knit supply chain and logistics events. A personal favorite early on was called the Supply Chain and Logistics Forum.

It was an intimate gathering onboard a cruise ship, a kind of floating "think tank" with a packed schedule, of private meetings with service providers, breakout groups with peers, plenary sessions with the industry's top leaders discussing the latest concerns, and networking socials.

It was a few days together, just far enough at sea to get the casino up and running, with morning-to-evening focus on all things supply chain and logistics.

There were also world-class keynote addresses. Among the ones that stand out for me was delivered by Gene Kranz, the NASA flight director famously portrayed by Ed Harris in *Apollo 13*. The man who coined the phrase "failure is not an option," and who led one of the most iconic examples of leadership under pressure in modern history.

I chose the Forum as my annual go-to event consistently for nearly a decade, before it eventually moved ashore, which I've still attended, but less regularly. When I was tasked with exploring opportunities to expand into Europe, I selected the one sailing out of Southampton, which gave me exposure to a broad cross-section of the supply chain industry throughout the continent.

Considering all the memories, there's one that stands above the rest, more personal than professional.

Not long after September 11, 2001, I attended one of these events. This one aboard the *Queen Elizabeth 2*. It was during the welcoming cocktail reception at the stern.

We were all gathered together as the ship began to pull away from the harbor. Right in front of us, the *Empire State Building* stood tall, lit up red, white, and blue. Not a dry eye.

A very personal moment, privately shared among the group. It's times like these that have a way of bonding people. These weren't just networking events; they became shared experiences, the kind of foundation that builds real relationships.

I count many friends from those days floating off the coast of New York and England's southern shores. Supply chain pirates, all in the same boat, all in search of the treasure map that would lead to business efficiencies and competitive advantage.

One final thought on managing and balancing the time you invest in professional development and networking. A great return on investment can be to engage with academia or continuing education. This usually doesn't require a major time commitment. It could be as simple as participating in one event per year.

For me, it involved two opportunities in Cambridge, Massachusetts, a collaborative supply chain program that brought together students, faculty, and industry leaders.

It began at Harvard, and later expanded, further developing at MIT. This exposure introduced me to some of the top minds in supply chain research and practice.

One leader in particular whom I developed a great deal of respect for is MIT Professor Yossi Sheffi.

My fondest memories date back to the release of his book, *The Resilient Enterprise*, published in 2005.

It was during that period I began attending events on campus. At the time, the global business community was still reflecting on SARS, a highly contagious and serious respiratory illness caused by a coronavirus similar to the one that causes COVID-19.

SARS had hit Mainland China and Hong Kong especially hard, along with several other Asian countries. Canada also saw a significant number of cases. The United States, by contrast, had relatively few. SARS offered a preview of how vulnerable the global supply chain could be, foreshadowing what we would see years later with COVID.

There were factory shutdowns, transport and logistics bottlenecks, international coordination was paralyzed by business travel restrictions. There were even early signs of just how exposed we were when it came to critical healthcare equipment and supplies that had long been offshored, without adequate supply contingency in the U.S. It was a wake-up call for supply chain leaders, and for industry more broadly.

American business, supply chain resilience, and national readiness during a health crisis were flagged as weak and concerning. Hence, the timely relevance of Professor Sheffi's book.

As it turns out, carrying the same force now as it did then.

I remember one conference where we simulated the projected outcomes of an avian flu outbreak, another scenario that mirrored real pandemic conditions.

Back then, the buzz was all about *resilience*. Building it into our supply chains was the emerging theme, and for me, this academic-industry venue became a great way to absorb practical insights I could use to mitigate risks in my own supply chain work. Looking back, it's clear that, as a country and as an industry, we failed to heed the call. COVID would confirm that in very profound ways.

There were other venues and opportunities that delivered real value, and I said "yes" to my fair share, balancing time and resources as best I could.

As my network grew, so did I, as a supply chain and logistics professional. The moral of the story? It relates back to something a mentor once told me, *one plus one equals more than two*. Putting yourself out there isn't easy for everyone. It doesn't come without sacrifice. Some people are drawn to the action, thrive under the spotlight, and seek center stage. That wasn't me.

However, by investing the time and energy, listening, observing, and accepting the challenges, it didn't take long before I found my footing, my professional moxie. I became confident enough to spark the conversation, share what was on my mind, and actively contribute as an industry collaborator.

That level of professional engagement can open doors for your career, expose you to cutting-edge research, grow your network, and prove personally rewarding in ways that last.

The key takeaway? Jump into the deep end. Pro tip, have a snazzy way to introduce yourself and your company, something professional but memorable, something that leaves a lasting impression.

For most of her childhood, when my daughter was asked what her dad did for a living, her go-to answer was, *"he makes candles."* Sometimes I'd even spin off a version of that. Not the only thing she taught me, for sure…just one of the early chart-toppers in her still-growing album of greatest hits.

NO AUTOPILOT FOR PROGRESS

Sharpening our instincts, honing our interpersonal skills, and expanding our networks, that's a powerful combination. For me, it hasn't just been impactful; it's made all the difference. But to what end, one might ask? Where are we really headed, and how will we recognize the moment we've arrived? Will we ever know when we've done enough, learned enough, or assembled the right mix of resources and relationships to call it complete? Or, is the truth simply that the work is never finished?

I'm reminded of one of my favorite movies, *Airplane*. In the scene that comes to mind, the captain faces a crisis, flips a switch, and out pops "Otto the Autopilot," a grinning inflatable who balloons to life and takes the controls.

Whatever happens next is in the hands of a cheerful stand-in who is, quite literally, full of hot air. Handing control to Otto looks like a solution, but in reality, it could steer you off course or straight into turbulence.

What played as slapstick in 1980 feels oddly relevant today, in an era when we're debating what it means to let AI take the controls. Beneath the humor lies a truth. There's no switch we can flip, no autopilot to carry us through.

What we can count on, instead, is the unexpected. The difference between Otto and real leadership is that someone still has to steer, and steering often means staying sharp, current, and willing to learn beyond your comfort zone.

That's a lesson I learned firsthand. Let me offer a personal example. I worked my way through law school as I was entering supply chain and logistics.

By the time I graduated, Compliance and Product Safety, along with overlaps in Quality Control and Assurance, had logically folded into my responsibilities, an unusual blend. Back then, wearing multiple hats was more the norm.

Being the one sent into the field to investigate product failures, study misuse, and analyze human factors became a surprising influence on how I thought about product development and supplier evaluations.

Years later, even with a law degree and more than twenty years of applied experience in compliance, I could still see the gaps. Concepts I'd only brushed against or best practices I knew of but hadn't mastered. To stay ahead, I enrolled in a program jointly led by Virginia Tech and the Society of Product Safety Professionals.

Harkening back to my earlier point about professional organizations, at this stage, I had been serving for many years as a consumer products subcommittee chair with ASTM (American Society for Testing and Materials), which provided views and influence over changes to product safety standards as a stakeholder.

However, as regulations shifted and scrutiny intensified, I felt the pull toward a more formal and tailored education, something that could sharpen my focus on what mattered most and help me apply it directly to my compliance work.

The Certified Product Safety Professional (CPSP) program wasn't built for beginners. Admission required years of experience and other qualifications, and the small cohorts reflected that. For me, it was exactly what I was looking for. The program turned into an incredible journey of learning and discovery, and the bonds I formed with colleagues have long outlasted the coursework itself.

One of the key takeaways was a glimpse into the future. Virginia Tech had been developing an AI-driven product-safety capability that aligned search terms to retrieve and categorize online consumer complaints. Organized the right way, that information would become an early warning system, revealing patterns of failure or misuse that could be addressed before problems multiplied.

It was, in a sense, a new kind of Otto. But this time, Otto wasn't destined to fly solo. He'd be a co-pilot. The yoke still in my hands, to guide how that intelligence is used and where to direct resources for earlier corrective, or even preemptive, action. And unlike his inflatable namesake, this Otto wasn't going to sit there grinning, he'd actually help keep the flight on course.

What mattered most wasn't the new technology itself, but how I chose to use it.

It was a reminder that staying current isn't a one-time task. It's a continuous choice. Change continues. Improvements never end. It may be said that "there's nothing new under the sun." But believe that too strongly, and you risk being left in the dark.

Change showed up again when Sustainability landed on my desk. For years I'd led green initiatives, mostly in formulation and packaging. This new mandate was different. The focus was on Zero Waste, something I knew little about. Once I dug in, I realized Zero Waste followed a hierarchy of preferences: eliminate, reduce, reuse, recycle. At its core, the essence of it all appeared more familiar than I originally thought.

Early in my career, I was mentored by some of the original Six Sigma black belts, veterans from Ford and GE who helped launch the movement in the 1980s. I was hardly certified then, more of an apprentice, serving in the role of a yellow or green belt, but the principles stuck with me long after those projects ended.

Over time, I kept using and refining those methods until I eventually earned certification as a Master Black Belt.

So, when Zero Waste came into focus, the best approach revealed itself quickly. Apply the DMAIC process:

Define, Measure, Analyze, Improve, Control.

Different challenge, same disciplined framework.

The DMAIC approach proved to be a strong foundation. I guided the team through value-stream mapping, failure mode and effects analysis, Pareto charts, and many other tools from the Six

Sigma playbook to generate ideas and develop waste-eliminating, landfill-diverting solutions.

However, as effective as we were, we kept falling short. It became clear we needed subject-matter expertise in Zero Waste best practices. At first, that meant bringing in consulting support, often the smartest move when gaps in capability appear. As the projects progressed, still rooted in Six Sigma principles but now enhanced by outside expertise, I once again felt the pull to deepen my own knowledge.

My instincts told me that sustainability was more than a passing initiative. With global attention mounting and expectations rising across the value chain, Zero Waste and other approaches to cutting greenhouse gas emissions were not just another change.

It was a transformation, one destined to shape a new business environment intent on making the environment we all depend on more sustainable for generations to come.

At the time, we chose Green Business Certification Inc.'s TRUE program to validate our Zero Waste performance once we met the diversion and process requirements.

GBCI also offered the "TRUE Advisor" program, an online education series covering best practices for applying the Zero Waste criteria, followed by an exam for credentialing.

Going through that program opened up an entirely new playbook. Suddenly, I had sharper tools to identify and trouble-shoot waste, and when combined with Six Sigma, the results accelerated. I was able to guide the team in new, adaptable ways.

Brainstorming sessions became richer. The ideas came from those closest to the work, and my role became shaping, connecting, and weaving those ideas into broader solutions. It was about casting vision, defining processes, and setting the path forward.

Eventually, I brought in staff with deeper expertise in Zero Waste and other environmental capabilities, including another TRUE Advisor. The solutions they've since developed go far beyond what I could have imagined.

My part was building the foundation that allowed the team to reach that potential, and then some. Over time, I stepped back from direct involvement, still accountable for results but relying on the team to keep us moving forward. The real strength was never in the framework alone, but in the team that brought it to life and carried us forward, trusted to play their positions while I stayed present, leaning forward and pushing us to go farther, to reach higher.

The idea I've tried to share through these examples is that supply chain and logistics live in a constant state of unfinished business. That doesn't mean projects don't get completed, goals achieved, or targets met. It means that once one bar is reached, the next one is set higher.

Change is the constant, expectations keep climbing, and customers will always want more than yesterday's best.

For me, staying sharp has meant continually investing in my own growth. It hasn't been the easiest path. It's tempting to hire a consultant for every project or a subject-matter expert for every gap, and sometimes that's necessary or a place to start.

More often, budgets don't allow for it. And even when they do, I've found it invaluable to learn alongside those experts, to absorb what I could and then decide whether the solution was a tool, a resource, or a role we needed to build into the long-term structure of the business.

ONE MORE TEST

We boarded our China Southern flight out of Los Angeles at 11 a.m., with a short connection in Guangzhou, and touched down in Ningbo just after 8 p.m. local time the following day, a journey of roughly 18 hours.

It was a quick ride to the new Sofitel in Yinzhou, with Dongqian Lake, sometimes called "Money Lake" for its round shape and legendary divine origins, glimmering nearby. We settled into the lobby lounge to prepare for the meeting ahead.

What had brought Jeff and Brad from quality and engineering with me on this trip was a technical issue uncovered in our internal testing. A flammable gas product showing test failures.

None had reached the market, but the discovery raised enough concern to warrant a direct meeting with the factory's technical team. By the time we arrived, the factory had already reviewed some preliminary information, and disagreed with our findings. They were convinced their quality control systems were airtight, that any problem must be unrelated to production.

The next morning, we climbed into the minivan sent to collect us and, less than an hour later, arrived at the factory. In the conference room, a team was waiting with product samples and a presentation queued up. Their report walked us through each checkpoint, standard, and test method, an earnest defense of their performance.

On that point, we agreed. The factory had earned its reputation for quality, and we had seen it firsthand over many years. Still, we had it on good authority that a problem did exist.

After the presentation, we agreed to take a closer look at the tooling, machines, and equipment used in production, and to run some tests onsite. It was time to get physical.

The first red flag appeared on the production floor, but it didn't tell the whole story. Eventually, we moved outside to a designated testing area for flammable products, set a safe distance from the plant and its workers.

That's where the real moment of clarity appeared. This was where surprise would sound, look, and register on confident faces, and where a eureka moment might break through.

First test: pass.

Second test: pass.

Third test: pass.

The proverbial third time's a charm seemed to be holding true, right before our eyes. Maybe our data, and our concern, wasn't as reliable as we thought.

Then, from the back of the group, a lone manager, brimming with confidence, leaned forward and said,

"One more."

The fourth test was set, and then—BANG.

Back to the conference room we went.

Same group, reassembled.

The factory's technical team sat with eyes cast down at the table. On the screen, the final slide of their earlier presentation still read, "Thank you!" A visible reminder of the hopeful mindset we all had when we walked out to the testing area.

The discussion that followed was different. It was candid, humble, and open. Together, with Jeff and Brad shoulder to shoulder with the factory's engineers, we got to the bottom of it.

And more importantly, we solved it.

The lesson that day reached beyond tooling and test data. Across oceans, cultures, and mindsets, we found that openness, curiosity, and humility often clear the path to real partnership.

Fortunately, years of trust and transparency gave us a foundation to build on. What we had uncovered wasn't something concealed or malicious, and no harm had been done. In fact, the redundancy in place, a pre-shipping inspection, had worked as intended. But what stalled progress at first was the unwillingness to accept that a problem could exist at all. Once that barrier came down, the solution became inevitable.

Even though we arrived in Ningbo convinced we had a problem, we nearly left with our minds changed, until a quiet voice called for one more test.

Just as important as the technical finding was the lesson in trusting instincts.

That can be tricky.

What happens when both sides hold firm,

each convinced their facts and intuition are right?

In my experience, that tension is more ordinary than exceptional. The challenge is breaking through the impasse with intention, and with enough grace and dignity to keep the partnership intact. We chose to follow the factory's lead with a listening ear, while keeping a keen eye on what we observed.

A small clue in the production area had already primed us for what surfaced outside during testing. Back in the conference room, it gave us a narrow path to the root cause. Had we seized on that discovery earlier as a "gotcha" or gone on the offensive, it would have pushed us farther apart. Instead, we let the process play out, together.

Instincts can be powerful, but they require the will to stand behind them, to let observations and insights give shape to the facts collected. Perspective, data, and analysis matter, but so does diplomacy. Striking that balance is never easy; it takes practice.

In the years that followed, our partnership with the factory only deepened. We pooled technical resources, co-wrote SOPs and testing protocols, and operated with a transparency that blurred almost every line of separation. Trust became stronger than ever. In time, we even achieved safety innovations that neither side could have reached alone, breakthroughs that grew directly from the clarity and humility sparked by the results of Test Four.

IN STEP WITH CURRENT

If the stories I've shared sparked new insight, offered a moment of clarity, or simply reminded you that leadership doesn't have to be perfect to be powerful, then this was worth our time. My hope is that they've given you something to reflect on, relate to, or build from as you shape your own approach.

Our journey together started with laughs and landed costs, and it ends with something both simpler and harder:

What it really means to keep moving forward.

In the end, what truly moves the needle isn't the title on your business card or the latest strategy framework, it's *you*.

Your mindset,

your presence,

your willingness to keep learning and evolving. That's the real advantage in any room you walk into.

The old adage that it's about who you know, or who knows you, certainly helps, *but knowing yourself matters more.*

You don't need to wait for a promotion, a bigger stage or someone else's permission to lead differently. You already hold the potential to change the atmosphere and direction,

in how you listen,

how you encourage,

how you respond, and

how you own your role,

both in the spotlight and when no one's watching.

Becoming the difference doesn't mean having all the answers; it means showing up with intention, humility, and a commitment to grow from every experience. It's choosing to lead with clarity when things are hectic,

to bring respect where there's tension, and

to model accountability without blame.

Keep investing in that version of yourself. Stay open. Stay aware, and keep moving toward the kind of leader the opportunity calls for. The most transformational force in any organization isn't only the process; *it's the person willing to lead with purpose.*

Challenge yourself when reaching a milestone to see it not only as a moment to celebrate, but an invitation to reach back and help someone else along.

Every professional, at some point, should embrace both sides of the journey, learning through being mentored with openness, and giving back through mentoring with care. That's how we build stronger teams, better industries, and lasting impact.

To lead well is to give generously,

develop continuously, and

know when to step back so others can rise,

create space for others to find their voice and

light a path for others to shine.

If you'll allow me to impart a few final words of wisdom, some things that pack light, easily carried with you on whatever adventure comes next:

- Wherever the journey leads, if a monkey with one-inch teeth smiles at you, it's best to smile back, while you carefully plan your exit.

- If you experience something shocking along the way, then hold a trophy while being chauffeured to your next stop, it's probably going to be a great trip after all.

- If the first thing you see when you land and step into a cab is a band of troll dolls and a bobblehead, buckle up and pay attention… whatever plays from the front seat might be more profound than you think.

- If you encounter a public-use thermometer, please put it under your arm, and nowhere else.

- If you have to stop the rickshaw to keep a promise, don't hesitate, even in the face of resistance you know in your gut is wrong.

- If you're in search of the inside track and haven't seen tin roofs or water buffalo, it's going to take reaching farther.

- If you have the chance to see more than you came for, chances are you'll be better for the experience.

- Even in the fog of overseas travel, don't let your guard down… there may be something piping hot that wasn't there a minute ago.

- If the Lazy Susan is spun your way, it's a great invitation to try something new.

- It pays to be mindful not to overlook a helpful ninja hiding in a business suit.

Finally,

when you find yourself navigating unfamiliar territory, somewhere far from home, whether on foot or behind the wheel, steady your course…

You're the big fish. Swim like it!

www.ingramcontent.com/pod-product-compliance
Lightning Source LLC
Chambersburg PA
CBHW070657190326
41458CB00053B/6922/J